From COP to CEO

How a bankrupt, broke street cop with a high school education and no business experience built a multi-million dollar real estate investment business that generated $500,000 cash in hand per year. He did it part-time, with no employees, out of a home office.

From COP to CEO

How a bankrupt, broke street cop with a high school education and no business experience built a multi-million dollar real estate investment business that generated $500,000 cash in hand per year. He did it part-time, with no employees, out of a home office.

By

Chuck Smith

Author's Note

The Difference between "Flipping" Property and "Quick Turning" Property

You've no doubt heard about "Flipping" properties in the media, and how it is a criminal act. "Flipping" a property involves fraud and the collusion of usually everyone involved in the deal. Those who engage in flipping "rig" an appraisal, so the value of the property to be sold is inflated. They will also present fraudulent information on unqualified buyers' mortgage applications, where the buyer appears to make more money, have better job stability and a better credit rating than they really do. Some of these crooks have even used children's Social Security numbers and invented credit to obtain loans.

I do not partake in, tolerate, or teach any of these practices.

What I teach is "Quick Turning" property. With skill and proper training, my students are taught how to find, fund and sell houses at lightning-fast speed for a mark up. We buy these properties at a deep, deep discount and sell them below market value, so there is never a question about the appraised value.

I just wanted to make that clear even before you start reading this book.

- Chuck Smith

Legal Notices

While all attempts have been made to verify information provided in this publication, neither the author nor the publisher assumes any responsibility for errors, omissions or contrary interpretation of the subject matter herein.

This publication is not intended for use as a source of legal or accounting advice. The publisher wants to stress that the information contained herein may be subject to varying state and/or local laws or regulations. All users of this manual are advised to retain competent counsel to determine what state and/or local laws or regulations may apply to the user's particular business.

The purchaser or reader of this publication assumes responsibility for the use of these materials and information. Adherence to all applicable laws and regulations, whether federal, state or local, governing professional licensing, business practices, advertising and all other aspects of doing business in the United States or any other jurisdiction, is the sole responsibility of the purchaser or reader. The author and publisher assume no responsibility or liability whatsoever on the behalf of any purchaser or reader of these materials.

Any perceived slights of specific people or organizations are unintentional.

Acknowledgements

To my beautiful wife, Amy—I have made a fortune in real estate, but the day I met you is the day I struck gold. Aside from being the best thing that has ever happened to me, you gave me four of the most precious gifts a man can have - our children. You've proven to be the most special of women: for years you were a cop's wife. Not knowing if you would see me alive at the end of my shift, you bravely stood by me. You were at my side when I attended the funerals of four other police officers killed in the line of duty. Those same officers we had just spent time with at parties, family functions and police gatherings. You stood along side me—not behind or in front of me—when I became involved in real estate. You helped me build a small fortune only to watch me lose it. Your belief in me never wavered, and I came back stronger, more motivated and even more successful. You now enjoy the fruits of our labor, and you deserve every bit of it.

To my first-born child, Chas, I love you so much for allowing me to experience just being a part of your life.

To my only daughter, Tara, you are no doubt Daddy's little girl. You know how to make this big tough guy melt to the gentleness of a lamb with a simple look. You hold a special place in my heart.

To my second youngest, Alex, when you were born, God gave you challenges. Those same challenges fueled my desire in real estate to accumulate wealth and cash flow to give you the best therapy money can buy. Because of you, when I grew tired, I never slowed down. When I hit a wall, I tore it down. When things became chaotic, I maintained control. You are such a beautiful young man. When you feel frustrated with the cards life has dealt you, know that you will rise above it all—because you can stand on my shoulders.

To my youngest, Sammy, you are the best buddy anyone could have. Your spirit is contagious.

To my father, Charles Sr. We are of two different personalities, but of the same mold. You instilled honesty and a work ethic like no other. My character and strength of will are, no doubt, due to your influence.

To my tough Irish mother, I owe my self-esteem. From my childhood until today, I have confidence to accomplish anything I set my mind to because of what you taught me.

To Dan Buxton, student, turned close friend. I feel I've learned as much from you as you have from me.

To my teacher, Ron LeGrand—as I told you a number of years ago, someday I'd be teaching real estate, so I can do a fraction, for others, of what you have done for me. Without your teachings, where would I be? You pointed me toward and showed me the correct path to get to the sunset. For your teachings, I will be forever grateful.

To my mentor and friend, John Ulmer, I thank you. My skill as a real estate investor has increased so much because of you. You are an educator and a role model. I am proud to call you my mentor and I am honored to call you my friend.

Finally, I'd like to thank America's Finest—The Police Officers. During my childhood, you were my heroes. Serving fifteen years among you is an experience I will always cherish. We went through doors together not knowing what was on the other side. Although I no longer wear the blue uniform, I was forever changed by the experience. The saying "once in, never out" holds true to this day. I thank you for the sacrifices you make every day; sacrifices I no longer have to make. I hope to achieve my goal of teaching as many cops as possible the investment strategies I use, so that they too can become wealthy. Every day you help others. Please allow me to help you and your family.

Table of Contents

Forward xv

Introduction Who Am I, and Why Am I Writing This? xxiii

Chapter 1 Growing up in Cleveland 26

Chapter 2 May the Force Be With Me (Becoming a Cop) 8

Chapter 3 More Experience on the Force 18

Chapter 4 My First Real Estate Experience 32

Chapter 5 The Decline and Fall of the Chuck Smith Empire 39

Chapter 6 My Second Real Estate Experience (Quite a
Difference!) 45

Chapter 7 Stories From Some of My Real Estate Deals (with
copies of checks) 52

Chapter 8 Overview of My Real Estate System 68

Chapter 9 Some of My Students' Success Stories (with copies of
checks) 101

Chapter 10 Asset Protection 115

Chapter 11 Personal Development 132

Chapter 12 Looking Toward the Future...................................... 141

DEFINITIONS OF REAL ESTATE TERMS............................. 161

REFERENCE SECTION 183

INDEX 185

Forward

by Dan S. Kennedy

I have spent 30 years of my life working intimately with entrepreneurs. Thousands of them. Many who started dumb, broke, even desperate, and went on to accomplish amazing things. My clients, coaching group members and close friends include people who've sold businesses they started on kitchen tables for as much as 130-million dollars. People who were literally homeless, living in relatives' basements or spare bedrooms, who now own million-dollar homes of their own. These people are quite unique when viewed against the bigger, broader population, yet there are far too many of them to accurately term any of them 'unique', especially if that implies they have some advantage you do not; that they may be able to do something you cannot.

Maybe you know me or know of me, as a result of my own books—nine at last count, including the recently up-dated NO B.S. BUSINESS SUCCESS BOOK or THE NEW PSYCHO-CYBERNETICS, or as result of my marketing oriented newsletter, NO B.S. MARKETING LETTER, or my speaking. Over 25 years, I spoke to over 200,000 people most years and frequently appeared on programs with former U.S. Presidents and world leaders, legendary entrepreneurs like Debbie Fields (Mrs. Fields Cookies), broadcasters Larry King and Paul Harvey, etc. I tell you these things about me, to let you know I have a long, diverse track record of assembling and disseminating experience-based, real-world information on money, business and success. I also practice what I preach: I have started, built, sold businesses successfully, invest in real estate and real estate based 'paper' as does the author of this book, and have been a self-employed, self-supporting entrepreneur nearly my entire life.

With all that said, I want to tell you about one of these many unique yet not unique entrepreneurs I've had the privilege of meeting, working with and being inspired by. The author of this book, Chuck Smith. And I want to tell you why you should very carefully and thoroughly digest every word he has written.

The reason I have used "No B.S." in many of my book titles and in my newsletter title is in reference to the unfortunate fact that there is so much b.s. shoveled into peoples' minds by fuzzy-headed academics, self-serving politicians, the liberal media, mis-guided ministers and, of course, people making money selling how-to-succeed information who have actually done nothing other than regurgitate someone else's information. When you decide you want to re-engineer your life, to be and have and achieve more, it is vitally important that you "consider the source."

I suggest to you the most worthy source is someone who has been where you are or worse off than you are, has accomplished what you aspire to, has legitimate real world in-the-trenches experience, has not forgotten from whence he came, and can share with you his experience. Ideas, theories, sometimes useful. But successful experience, priceless.

It is for this reason that I was so impressed with Chuck the first time I met him. I was speaking at a conference for what we call "information marketers', and heard Chuck tell an abbreviated version of his story you will read in detail in this book, and heard him describe his hopes for converting his hard-fought experience into books, courses and seminars that could help others. But what made Chuck stand out from hundreds of others in that same room also eager to create and market their own information products was that Chuck had arrived at a "success plan" replicatable by others 100% from actual experience, and had achieved considerable wealth, independence, security and desirable lifestyle from an unlikely, disadvantageous starting point. This is the stuff of great entrepreneurial success stories. This is the right foundation for a man, mission and information that is of real value and worth to others. I have done everything in my power to encourage him, and to direct him to productive paths. I had a little something to do with the book now in your hands and with the way it is written.

Chuck Smith is one of those true-life symbols that free enterprise, capitalism and personal initiative work and can work for anyone who will work.

I often say there's virtually no excuse to be broke in America. As the late comedian Sam Kineson used to say, "If you aren't going to make it here - where?". Chuck Smith is living proof this statement is true. He was a low paid street cop who overcame obstacles including bankruptcy and ruined credit to quickly - note I said quickly - create $100,000.00, then $500,000.00, then $1,000,000.00 in yearly real, cash income for his family, starting with nothing more than useful information, a reasonable plan, initiative, personal responsibility, self-motivation. If he can do it, why can't you? Or anyone else? There's also no excuse to work in a job, stay mired in a business or live a life that does not excite and satisfy you. Chuck Smith is living proof that statement is also true.

<u>His book is really three books in one</u>. It is his story, his, if you will, "blue" rags to riches story. It should drive home to you the truth that anything you wish to achieve financially and in terms of lifestyle is readily accessible to you, regardless of where you are now. It should provide what from-scratch billionaire W. Clement Stone, in his great book 'The Success System That Never Fails', called INSPIRATION TO ACTION.

His book is also a clear, straightforward overview of Chuck's replicatable "success plan" and a behind the scenes look at his business. You will see that what he does you can do, how he makes his money just about anyone can copy. Of notable importance, you will see abundant evidence that his "plan" yields real results.

Chuck is, after all, a former cop, so you should expect evidence from him. This should give you what I call CONFIDENCE TO ACTION.

<u>His book is also, frankly, a sales pitch.</u> That is, in part, the result of my urging. It tells you what to do next and how Chuck can and will help you. This is a spectacular opportunity. For most people, it never occurs; an 'ordinary' wage earner who becomes a millionaire and is willing, even eager to take you under his wing and show you everything he does and how he does it. I view this book's #1 job as making a strong sales pitch - selling you on the idea of greater success, selling you on you and the truth that you can do it, selling you on the "success plan" you can use, and

selling you on getting off your duff, into action, with Chuck's direction and assistance.

<u>Oh, and one other thing, about getting rich quick.</u> All your life you've been counseled and cautioned against get-rich-quick schemes. This counsel has come from people who are clueless about getting rich, quick, slow or any other way. Remember what I said about: consider the source. People iike Chuck know you can create very rapid, dramatic, gigantic improvements in your financial life because he has done so himself. He is a worthy source. There's no virtue in getting rich slow. There's no rule against quick. As you read this book, you might give special consideration to the idea of speed.

One of the great success educators, Earl Nightingale, observed that most highly successful people hit a time and place in their lives where they accomplish more in 2 years than they did in the previous 20. I have personally found that to be true, and I have observed it countless times. Chuck has lived it as well. So can you. It occurs for a person because of the convergence of many factors. Two big ones are readiness and the discovery of a valid blueprint, a workable plan, often with the support and encouragement of a beneficent mentor. One of those important factors is right here for the taking. The other is entirely within your personal control.

All positive change occurs in movement through three steps: one, Awareness; two, Decision; three, Action. Chuck Smith's book will make you aware of what can be done, how it's done and provide ample evidence you can do it too.

If you happen to be a police officer, firefighter, rescue worker, or member of the military reading this, Chuck's background and story should have special meaning for you. You work in jobs that, quite honestly, I would never do for love nor money. You put yourself at risk for my benefit, others' benefit, society's benefit. You are woefully underpaid. That is not going to change. Nike is not going to suddenly start handing out 90-million shoe contracts to cops. You can bitterly complain about how unfair all this is over your beer or you can do something about it.

Not something to change the system or society's priorities. Something personal, practical, direct and productive.

You can continue serving as Chuck did, while investing some off-hours time in a very different field, where enormous financial rewards from honest, ethical, safe work awaits. You can develop and profit from your brain rather than your brawn. You can profit from leverage rather than manual labor. You will naturally be far more skeptical than people in other occupations. You may be sorely tempted to shrug Chuck's story off as fluke, as freak accident, as lucky break, or as result of some mysterious talents you do not possess. You will even question the evidence. It's perfectly okay to have such doubts, as long as they do not rise to the level of paralysis. There's a saying: a wise man investigates what a fool takes for granted. I urge you not to let your past experience determine your future.

Chuck is, above all else, a sincere individual. I am sure that will come through loud and clear to you just as it has to me. That is a quality in alarmingly short supply these days. In short, he is a No B.S. guy with a No B.S. success plan. My kind of guy.

Dan S. Kennedy
www.dankennedy.com
www.renegademillionaire.com

Introduction
Who Am I, and Why Am I Writing This?

I used to be a cop. I'm not one anymore, but for more than fifteen years law enforcement was the center of my life. I liked the feeling of serving my community, the camaraderie of being around my brother and sister officers and even, sometimes, the danger, the rough-and-tumble action of it.

I liked less the politics, and the bias and intolerance I saw within the department. In any organization, you're going to have politics; I guess it's the nature of people to be that way. I'm a "straight-ahead" kind of guy: I say what I mean, and I mean what I say. I don't really have the temperament to deal with the game-players and the politicians, or the self-promoters who will climb the social or corporate ladder at the expense of everyone around them. I'd rather be involved in something positive, and toward the end of my law enforcement career that was getting more and more difficult to do.

I came from a blue-collar background, as did my family. My mom and dad never went to school past the eighth grade—college was almost unheard of in my neighborhood. Honesty and a strong work ethic were instilled in me from an early age.

I grew up in a pretty rough neighborhood of Cleveland, Ohio. Career choices were limited: you could go on welfare, become a gangster or a criminal, try the military, or go into law enforcement. I chose law enforcement, and for many years it worked out ok for me. Not spectacular, but ok.

I rose through the ranks, becoming a Sergeant at age 29. I saw some unbelievable things, both good and bad, during my time on the force. I witnessed first hand how cruel and destructive people can act towards one another, and how heroic and kind others can be. I saw good friends die in the line of duty, and suffered numerous injuries myself.

When I was thirty, married with four kids, I began looking around for something that would provide my family with a little more stability and financial success. You can't provide many of the luxuries of life on a cop's salary. Sometimes, you even have trouble providing the *basics*, especially if you have a child with special needs, as we did. I tried working second jobs, or 16-hour shifts with the department, and was miserable. Not only was I exhausted, but it took me away from my family much more than I wanted.

Real estate had always interested me. I thought I might buy a few houses, become a landlord—with the houses rented I'd have a positive cash flow, and the properties would be like money in the bank, increasing in value every year and giving my family some much-needed security. I saw it as a way to provide me with a second career, and perhaps allow me to generate that extra income for my family so I could give them the things that I wanted. I found a mentor, and began investing. I was really aggressive – within 12 months I owned 43 rental properties, and had a net worth of over 1 million dollars.

Then I lost it all.

I knew nothing about protecting my assets, and I got sued by a tenant, who claimed her son had gotten hurt on one of my properties. A trip through the justice system resulted in her obtaining a large judgment against me, and her attorney started picking off my properties one by one. Like a house of cards, my world came crashing down around my ears. My wife and I were left with the house we lived in, and we had to file bankruptcy to protect that.

Real estate had given me a glimpse of what could be, then the door had slammed shut with a vengeance. I was *worse* off than I was before I began investing, because now my credit was ruined by the bankruptcy. I looked around at the ruins of my life and wondered: *Now what in the hell am I going to do?*

Giving up wasn't an option. I had a family to support. Bills to pay. I had only one choice: rebuild my life. At that point, I didn't have the foggiest idea of how I was going to do it; I just knew that it must be done.

And as strange as it sounds, I still believed that real estate was the answer. Don't ask me why – I just felt sure down to my bones that there had to be a way for real estate to provide the things I wanted in my life, and the things my family needed. I just had to find it. *And I did.* And I can show you how to do the same.

Many people work much of their lives as drones: they get up in the morning, go to a job they really don't like, for wages that really don't cut it – that's why most families have to have two incomes just to survive these days. They'll work for years for people or organizations they dislike, with little or no hope of improving their lot, simply because that's what most of the people in this country do. It's easier than accepting responsibility for their own lives, because then they can play the "blame game". They can't do this, because of that; or they can't start their own business like they've always wanted because they need a steady paycheck. Paycheck to paycheck survival breeds depression. Believe me, I know. And most people can't, *or won't*, lift a finger to find their way out of that trap.

The whole reason I wanted to write this book is to show you a better way. To prove to you that it never pays to give up – that you *can* have financial success and create the kind of life you've always wanted. Money in the bank? Absolutely. Vacations in Bermuda? Sure, if that's what you want. Travel, security, college for the kids – however you define success, you can have it. But you have to listen and learn first. ***Then you have to act.*** This is one man's story of success, failure and redemption. Mine. I want to share with you what worked for me, and can work for you, if you take the time and effort to implement it. So buckle your seatbelts and hang on, because it's been one helluva ride!

Chuck Smith
August 2003

"A hard beginning makes a good ending."
-John Heywood

Chapter 1
Growing up in Cleveland

I grew up in a rough part of Cleveland, Ohio. Born in 1964, I was the second child in a family that was a prime example of the American middle class: blue- collar, hard working, never enough money for the luxuries in life. We had a roof over our heads, food on the table and clothes to wear, and we counted ourselves lucky to have that much.

Not that I had a bad childhood; my parents were hard-working and honest, and they provided my sister and brother and me with a stable and loving home. Neither my mom or dad had gone to school past the eighth grade—they lived in a time and came from a culture when higher education was not only out of reach, but considered an extravagance. It was more important to learn a trade and bring in money to help the family, which is what they did. My dad worked as a machinist in a factory, as did my mom. It was hard work, and just like nowadays, hard to raise a family when both parents have to work.

My brother and sister and I were "latchkey" kids before the term became popular. We quickly learned to fend for ourselves after school, coming home, doing homework and chores and watching TV. It's a wonder we didn't get in anymore trouble than we did, but we were essentially good kids. We had a few minor scrapes, but nothing serious.

We lived in the East 55th & Woodland area of Cleveland, a working class neighborhood that just bordered the projects. It's also known as the Cleveland Police Department's Fourth District, and it had one of the highest crime rates in the city. At least it did when I lived there. It was a patchwork neighborhood of post-World War II homes, mom-and-pop stores, urban blight and tenement housing; rusted-out cars next to houses with neatly-kept lawns; drug dealers and prostitutes peddling their wares, cop cars and ambulances with lights flashing and sirens screaming a common sight; unemployed men gathering in groups in front of empty storefronts, or on street corners - bored, frustrated, looking for trouble or sometimes work, usually in that order.

It was an ethnically diverse neighborhood, as was the entire city of Cleveland. Founded in 1796 by an American Revolutionary Brigadier General by the name of Moses Cleaveland, the spelling of the city was later changed to "Cleveland", either by mistake or as a way to fit the word on a newspaper masthead—no one seems to know the real reason. From its beginnings as a frontier village, it quickly grew into a manufacturing and business center for Northern Ohio, drawing immigrants from the east in large numbers.

Hungarians, Irish, Armenians, Germans, Hispanics, African Americans, American Indians, Italians – virtually every ethnic group in American was represented at one time or another. It was a real "melting pot".

As each ethnic group would rotate through the neighborhoods, they'd bring their own culture and language, customs and prejudices. They'd marry, find jobs or open businesses, begin to raise families, do well or poorly, depending on their own brand of luck and determination, then they'd typically move on, opening the way for the next group to roll through. Each group would leave the neighborhood a little more worn, a little more in need of repair. The whole area was in a downward spiral that's almost impossible to stop, unless the government gets involved with community revival programs and a huge infusion of cash, and at that time, neither of those things was going to happen.

Those "lazy, crazy, hazy" days of the 60's weren't really in evidence in my neighborhood when I was growing up. Crime was a real problem in Cleveland at that time. Free love and peaceful protests weren't the order of the day. With a population nearing 500,000, only Dayton, which actually had about one half the population of Cleveland, had a higher crime rate. Violent and property crimes abounded: murder, forcible rape, aggravated assault, burglaries - all ranked among the highest levels in the state.

Analysts figure there's all kinds of reasons why crime goes up in urban populations: too many people living in too small an area, high unemployment figures, poverty, inadequate education, no hope. That last one is probably the biggest factor, because people with no hope have nothing to lose. They figure *"Why not? Who's gonna care?"* Whatever the rationale, all of those factors were present in my neighborhood, and it made for a rough situation. I was a skinny kid, small for my age, which posed a problem when it came to hanging out with my friends or even attending school. Older, bigger kids tend to pick on you when they perceive you as a quarry that's younger, smaller and weaker than they are. My only saving grace was I was quicker, and scrappy. I had my share of dust-ups and fights – I'd win some, lose some. My mom hated for me to fight, coming home with a bloody nose or scrapes and bruises, but she knew what kind of neighborhood we lived in, so she was well aware of what I faced.

I attended Central Junior High School, located at East 40th and Central Ave., right in the heart of the projects. In some ways, junior high was worse than high school, in terms of the amount of social chaos and actual physical danger. At that age, boys especially are testing the limits of their boundaries, fighting for their place in the food chain and to establish their dominance in the pecking order.

School was less an educational experience than a form of running guerilla warfare: sudden physical attacks followed by disciplinary action if you were caught, gleeful relief if you'd gotten away with it. Any kid alone was a target; you had to have friends to watch your back. Add to that indifferent teachers, students out of control in the classrooms, and a school that was dilapidated and coming apart at the seams, and you have a situation that's ripe for abuses. We used to think the rats were dogs, until we realized they didn't bark! Just kidding, but just barely.

Then I discovered martial arts. Martial arts was a way for me to use my size and agility to my advantage; it taught me restraint and a sense of fearlessness when confronted by a bigger, stronger opponent. I liked the discipline of the

4

classes, the comfortable routine of practice, and, most importantly, I liked the feeling of competency it gave me. I was always pretty good at handling myself, but learning the skills of martial arts gave me an additional boost of self-confidence. In fact, I enjoyed it so much I competed at events all throughout my junior high and high school years, and continued into my years on the police force. I earned my first black belt at age 18, and in 1989 I competed at the Police Olympics, and won a bronze medal for my department in my discipline.

As tough as it was, life in my neighborhood prepared me for becoming a cop later in life. I saw some horrific things growing up, and the violent crime statistics of Cleveland weren't just numbers to me—the violence touched my own family.

My aunt was raped when I was about nine years old during what we would now call a home invasion robbery. Two guys followed my uncle home and forced their way into the house. Over a period of about 7 hours they repeatedly raped my aunt in front of her husband and children. I can remember we were going to go visit her, and we drove by her house while this was going on, but didn't stop because the blinds were drawn and we didn't think she was home. A neighbor later called the Cleveland Police, who caught the suspects in the house.

We also had a close family friend that was murdered. His name was Chuck Mitchell, and he and my dad were very close. I recall that he lived in the Collinwood section of Cleveland, where George Clooney starred in the movie "Welcome to Collinwood". At any rate, I was about 16 years old when he was killed; I remember that because he used to give me a ride to my driver's education class. Chuck was walking out of a local tavern when, according to witnesses, a car pulled up and someone started shooting. Chuck fell next to his car, and the suspect walked up and shot him twice more in the head at point-blank range. And I wasn't exempt from the violence, either. At age thirteen, I was stabbed in a street fight that came out of nowhere. I was walking down the street with a friend of mine, minding our own business, when this guy about 20 years old walks up and starts arguing with my buddy. The next thing I know is this guy is challenging me to a fight. He picks up a broken Pepsi bottle (back then they were glass) and proceeds to jam it into my leg. It all happened so fast I didn't realize I'd been stabbed; I just remember the feeling of warm blood running down my leg, and asking myself "why did this guy use a weapon?" He was bigger and stronger than I was – he didn't need the extra advantage of a weapon. After he stabbed me he punched me several times in the face, and then took off running. I was lying on the ground, half unconscious, and could hear the sirens from the Cleveland Police cars screaming in my direction before they flooded the area, pulling up around me and my buddy. I received seven stitches in my leg, a broken cheekbone and the knowledge that violence could happen anywhere, anytime, to anybody.

From an early age, I knew that life was a precious thing, and fleeting. We lived in a dangerous and deadly time, and nothing could be taken for granted, least of all tomorrow.

My father instilled a strong work ethic in me. His motto was: *a little hard work never hurt anybody*. Nothing was ever handed to me on a silver platter. If I wanted something I was encouraged to go out and earn the money to get it on my own. I almost always had a part-time job as I went through school; in fact, when I was thirteen, I forged my birth certificate so I could get a job as a busboy at the mall. I worked all sorts of jobs: fast food, restaurants, places like that. Nothing that paid any real money, but it brought in a little bit, enough to help me buy some of the things I wanted. I realized at about the age of eight or nine that I wanted to be a cop—truthfully, outside of my immediate family members, Cleveland police officers were the only heroes I had. They seemed invincible: they were tough, they were competent and they could bring order to any chaotic circumstances, no matter how desperate. When someone was murdered and the surrounding neighbors disappeared behind locked doors and closed curtains, the police would show up, calm, stoic and in control of the situation.

In my years on the force I saw the best and the worst of them, and to this day, I believe in my heart of hearts that they do one of the most difficult and dangerous jobs on the face of the earth, and most of them do it with class and dignity under the most trying of circumstances.

When I was about eight years old, I remember sitting on the front porch of our house talking with my father, and telling him I wanted to be a cop. I told him I wasn't sure what kind of cop I wanted to be, meaning detective, patrol cop, SWAT team cop, etc. He looked at me and said "Son, be the type of cop you would want working in your neighborhood, where your family lives."

It was a code I would live by from the time I put on a badge until the day I gave it back and retired from the force.

"Troubles are often the tools by which God fashions us for better things."
Henry Ward Beecher

Chapter 2
May the Force Be With Me (Becoming a Cop)

It takes a special breed of person to become a cop—to go through doors not knowing what's on the other side; to respond to murder scenes and domestic disturbances and gruesome traffic accidents without losing your own essential humanity and compassion; to really and truly believe you're there "to protect and serve", takes a rare human being.

From the time I was small I knew I wanted to join the force; unfortunately the Police departments in the Cleveland area all had a minimum hiring age which was twenty one. After I graduated from high school, I worked a variety of jobs while taking some college courses. I never obtained a college degree of any sort, largely because, other than law enforcement, nothing struck a spark with me and made me want to turn it into a career. I finally settled into a job as a security guard, which was as close as I could get to being a cop at that age. I was pretty much biding my time until I was old enough to apply for a job with the department.

Many large metropolitan police agencies go through various formations and incarnations in their history before arriving at their present structures, and the one I went to work for was no different. From a small frontier town with an elected city marshal assisted by a few constables and volunteer night watchman, the department experienced typical growing pains as it struggled to keep pace with the growth of the city around it. The very first "official" police department of the city had one superintendent, six officers and twenty nine patrol officers to protect the city's 67,000 inhabitants—a far cry from today's statistics.

A safety director was appointed, in the pre-World War II days, to oversee the reorganization and restructuring of the department, and promptly abolished the existing precinct system, replacing it with police "districts"; each commanded by a captain. That system remains largely in place today, although, of course, with a much larger police force protecting a much larger population.

Shortly after my twenty-first birthday I applied to one of the Cleveland area departments and was accepted as a candidate. I entered the police academy at twenty-two and was soon out on the street in my uniform, ready to join my "brothers and sisters in blue" in protecting and serving my community. I was proud and apprehensive, scared and pleased, anxious and confident all at the same time, and very sure that I was living my dream.

I started off, as many officers do, as a patrol cop responding to any and all calls for assistance: bar fights, traffic stops, arrest warrants, search warrants, drug busts; you name it, we rolled on it. I got to know the bad sections of town: where the drug dealers hung out, where the pimps and prostitutes plied their wares; the bars where people were most likely to get stabbed or shot. There were some streets we went down where we wished we'd had bullet-proof cars, or maybe even a tank or two. If this was a war zone, we were the front-line troops.

The Cleveland metropolitan area in the 1980's was no different from a lot of major urban areas in the United States with an exploding drug problem and a corresponding rise in crime rates. When I first joined the force, the crack cocaine wars were in full swing.

Most people don't realize that drug use in this country has kind of arrived in waves. The first wave hit back in the nineteenth century, largely started by Chinese immigrants who came to work in the gold mines and build the railroads. They brought opium with them, and over the next twenty years or so opium dens moved steadily eastward, and the number of people who became addicted progressively increased. Medicine was relatively primitive at that point, and doctors gratefully used any of the opiates available: morphine, laudanum (alcohol suffused with opium), paregoric (alcohol, opium and camphor) and codeine, to treat their patients.

When people, and local governments in particular, became aware of just how big a problem drug addiction could be, they began to recognize something needed to be done about both the addicts and the drugs themselves. In 1875, San Francisco became the first city in America to pass an anti-drug law. The Federal government got into the act, and became an international leader in the movement to restrict addicting drugs solely to medical use. By the beginning of World War II, illegal drug use was mostly considered a social ill that had been solved.

The 1960's saw a resurgence of drug use, from marijuana to amphetamines to psychedelics. That was part of "being cool" at that time: smoke a little weed, pop a few pills, what's the harm? The 1970's and 80's was where things really got ugly, with the reappearance of cocaine.

Powder cocaine trafficking reached kind of a peak in the mid 1980's, when it was estimated some six million Americans were regular users. The myth being circulated at that time was that it was a "high-end" drug: expensive, something of a status symbol and with no serious consequences. Little did they know.

Toward the mid to late '80's, crack cocaine made its appearance, and drug dealers used a different marketing technique: they focused on traditional inner-city drug users. Crack was relatively cheap in comparison to powder cocaine and could be smoked—users had no idea how intensely addictive it could be. I've known dealers who would give away "free samples" to new customers just to get them hooked. It can work that quickly.

Columbian drug cartels smuggled cocaine in literally by the ton, and became rich beyond anyone's dreams of avarice. When money's involved, especially when it's *large* amounts of money and illegal activity, you're gonna have problems. Big problems! Turf wars erupted as wholesalers and dealers fought for territory over who had the right to sell this crap on which street corner. What made it really scary was for the first time, high-powered automatic weapons came into play. Tech-9's (9 millimeter pistols), converted to fully-automatic, could fire entire clips of 30 rounds in less than 15 seconds. Human life ceased to have any meaning in this kind of war: wholesale carnage became the order of the day. I've seen twelve and thirteen year old kids hosed down on street corners by kids not much older. "Drive-by's" became a new phrase in our vocabulary, and everyone understood what it meant. Innocent bystanders killed because they happened to be in the wrong place at the wrong time; babies, grandmothers, people waiting for buses, all killed because some little punk overshot his intended victim. And unlike TV or the movies, these people had families: moms, dads, sisters, cousins, that cared about them and whose lives were wrecked because of the escalating violence. I've seen more people destroyed by crack cocaine than almost anything else I can think of. Drug dealers have a lot to answer for.

So when I first hit the streets, it really *was* like going into a war zone. You honestly never knew if today was the day you were going to get caught in the middle of a gun battle between warring drug dealers. Police officers live with that kind of uncertainty every day, but this was in the extreme. The rank-and-file felt that we were outgunned and out manned. It was certainly a case of "us" against "them" mentality. There were more of them than there were of us, and they had more firepower.

Still, even with the danger, I loved police work. I quickly gained a reputation as a proactive honest cop among my peers, and I worked hard to maintain that standing. I wanted to be known, and I was, as a cop that could be counted on when it mattered. They say "once in, never out" of police officers, and that's really true. There are bonds forged under those kinds of circumstances that are almost impossible to break.

You know, I believed at that time, and I still do, that you could double or triple the amount of money we give our police officers and still not come close to paying them what they're worth, in terms of the sacrifices they make and the risks they run on a daily basis.

Like a lot of officers, I worked long hours, pulling double shifts and quickly gaining experience on the streets. Cops see things every day that can twist their view of the world and turn them cynical and jaded. The trick is to let the bad stuff roll off your back and remember the things that are positive about your encounters with people. Sometimes that's hard to do.

My partner and I got called to a man threatening suicide call one day. We pulled up in front of his house; decent house, decent neighborhood, everything looked pretty calm. We walked up to the door, it opens, and this guy is standing there with a gun to his head. We follow him back into his kitchen, trying to talk to him, to find out what the problem is; all the time he's got the gun pointed right at his temple. Turns out he's really depressed and distraught: his wife died, his mom just died, he's got no one left to take care of him, he's lost all hope that anything is ever going to be right in his life again. We tried to convince him that he was wrong, that there *was* still hope, that we would get him some help, but he kept shaking his head "no", and then right in the middle of our conversation, he pulls the trigger. When people lose hope, they lose everything. They can't see anything but darkness in front of them, no light, no optimism, no relief. Just despair. It's a horrible thing to watch. Two feet away from the guy, and there was nothing I could do to stop him. He fell on the floor of his kitchen, and I held his hand as he died. That's all I could do for this poor guy.

My experiences weren't *all* bad. The department felt like I had potential and considered me for a detective position after only two years on the job, which was pretty unusual. I was interested, but the problem was, at that time budget cuts and departmental reorganizations were on the table and by the time all the reshuffling was done, there were no detective positions open.

It was around this time that the best thing that every happened to me happened: I met my future wife Amy. She's the light of my life, and it took me a while to talk her into taking a chance on this beat-up street cop. She did though, even though I know her fear was sometimes overwhelming her. A cop's spouse lives with a very private kind of terror— never knowing if their husband or wife will return home at the end of the shift. Amy stood by me during the best of times and the worst. She's been at my side as we attended the funerals of four other police officers that were killed in the line of duty; cops she knew from parties, family functions and police gatherings. I could be next. She knew that and accepted it. Well, maybe not accepted it, but knew the risks.

Anyway, we got married when I was twenty-five. I was so happy and so proud that this beautiful woman had agreed to share her life with me. I was young and strong, doing a job I loved, with the woman I loved beside me. What more could life offer? How could it get any better?

But it did. Babies started arriving; beautiful children; three boys and a girl—the most precious gifts any parent can have. We moved to a bigger house to accommodate our growing family. I could foresee nothing but wonderful things for the future. This was going to be our happily ever after. Dreams really did come true.

Then our third child was diagnosed as being mildly autistic. We were stunned, and like most parents, knew virtually nothing about autism. Autism is a widely misunderstood neurological disorder that affects the brain, usually in the areas of communication and social skills. Children with autism can display a wide range of symptoms and characteristics, but unlike some neurological disorders there's no specific test to determine autism.

Many professionals, even in the medical and educational field, don't understand how autism can affect people, and how they can best work with autistic children. Like any child, autistic children will respond in both negative and positive ways to their environment. They're still individuals; they have their own personality and characteristics, just like any other person. Alex was our son; we loved him and would do whatever was necessary to help him over this hurdle.

If anything, knowing my son had special needs only served to motivate me to provide a better life for my family. Special education classes and medical needs presented new challenges, and I was up to the task. I worked even harder than I had before—more shifts with the department, taking second jobs to bring in more income. Even though it took me away from my family much more than I wanted, I was glad to do it if it would help my son. That's what parents do: they provide for their kids.

So even though this little cloud had developed on our horizon, our lives were still pretty sweet. My work at the department was going well, I still liked what I did for a living and I had received a number of commendations for bravery over the years.

One was from the Ohio House of Representatives, for pulling a lady out of a burning car. We had responded to a report of an accident and arrived on the scene to find this lady seriously injured and unconscious behind the wheel of her smashed car, which was already on fire. I pulled her out, and my partner and I carried her to the side of the road, while her car continued to burn behind us. Just two minutes later, the car blew up—just like something out of the movies. It was unbelievable.

Another time my partner and I arrested a fugitive murder suspect from Detroit, who was accused of killing a woman and her two year old child. We received a commendation from the Cuyahoga County Prosecutor's Office for that one.

Police work was still the most rewarding, frustrating and agonizing work that I could ever imagine doing. We saw things every day that either ripped your heart right out of your chest, or made you shake your head at the ironies of life.

One night I stopped at a pay phone to call my wife—back then we didn't have cell phones. As I was talking to her, a motorcycle came down the street behind me and I idly turned to watch it go past. It was moving at a good rate of speed—I guess the driver was trying to impress his girlfriend who was on the back. Anyway, as I watched, the motorcycle went out of control and slid into a street sign. I guess the guy must have hit it just right because it decapitated him. I stood there, stunned, then said to my wife, "Gotta go, honey. A motorcycle just wrecked in front of me, and the guy's head is rolling around in the street." She still can't believe to this day that it happened while I was talking to her.

Another time we got called to a house by a report of a baby not breathing. This was about three o'clock in the morning. All police officers are trained as first responders, so we know CPR and rescue breathing, first aid and childbirth and all that stuff. And even though we used our training from time to time, all cops will tell you getting called to a child injury or a child not breathing is one of the most traumatic calls you can ever get. Anyway, we rushed into this house, and the mother's hysterical: her baby's not breathing and she doesn't know what to do. We tried CPR until the paramedics arrived, with no response. We couldn't get a pulse, no breathing, we couldn't get the baby to respond in any way. The paramedics didn't have any better luck—they loaded the baby in the ambulance and took off lights and sirens screaming for the hospital. But we heard later the child was declared dead on arrival. Here's a bunch of tough-guys cops, standing around with tears in their eyes because we'd been asked to help and there was nothing we could do.

I was so shook up, so rattled, that as we left the scene, I found a pay phone and pulled my cruiser over so I could call my wife. Our son was about three months old then, and I woke Amy up in the middle of the night and made her go check on him, just to make sure he was ok. That's how deeply it affected me. And I know a lot of the cops that were on that scene that night probably did the same thing.

There *were* positive things that happened, though. At age 29, I was promoted to Sergeant. I'd been a cop about eight years, and I really felt like my career was on-track. I could easily see myself doing police work for the foreseeable future: climbing the department ladder step by step, going for a Lieutenant's position, or even Captain in the future. How about considering Detective again? Nothing felt out of reach.

*People who soar are those who refuse to sit back, sigh and wish
things would change. They neither complain of their lot nor
passively dream of some distant ship coming in. Rather, they
visualize in their minds that they are not quitters; they will not
allow life's circumstances to push them down and hold them
under.*
- Charles Swindoll

Chapter 3
More Experience on the Force

Being a street cop is a lot of hard work. I'm not just
talking about the mental or psychological aspect of it; that's
hard enough, but I mean it's *physically* hard work. It's
demanding and can be exhausting: chasing down
suspects—literally chasing them down in foot races;
subduing violent felons or people who are mentally unstable;
struggling with drunks—all of that takes conditioning and
stamina. When you include the psychological pressures of
the job, it's no wonder cops get burned out at a rate that
exceeds most other professions.

Experience counts, don't get me wrong. It's absolutely
critical to have officers on the street that have been around
the block a time or two—a seasoned officer can provide a
calm and deliberate style of leadership that is vital to good
police work. But make no mistake about it ... street work is
for the young.

During my career on the force, I sustained more injuries
than a pro football player. I've been punched, kicked, barfed
on, stuck with a hypodermic needle, blew my knee out,
injured my back and been thrown down three flights of stairs.
Like I said, it's a job for the young.

In 1999 I tore the rotator cuff in my shoulder and had to go in for surgery. At about the same time, Kenny Lofton, center fielder for the Cleveland Indians, was undergoing the same surgery after he tore *his* rotator cuff sliding into home plate. I remember laying there in my hospital bed, watching all the media coverage of Kenny and how the hospital and doctors treated him like royalty simply because he was a celebrity and a sports figure, and feeling disgruntled because I was having to fight and argue and struggle with the worker's compensation carrier just to get them to pay for my surgery, even though I'd been injured in the line of duty. It wasn't fair or equal treatment, but sometimes that's just the way things are. But it still bothered me.

As my injuries mounted over the years, I started looking around for the first time at doing something other than police work. As I moved up in the ranks, I realized that at some point I'd be moving away from street work and more toward a desk job. And with a desk job comes not only more pay and more responsibility, but also more politics.

I've never been particularly good at playing politics—I'm too straightforward and plain-spoken. My personal style is to be blunt and honest, and that doesn't always sit well with higher-ups. I can't soft-pedal answers or double speak just to make points with a boss; I get impatient and aggravated with people who can't handle the plain, unvarnished truth. So, even though I was popular and well-liked by my brother and sister officers, I was viewed with a somewhat jaundiced eye by my supervisors. Not that this really upset me—all in all, I'm more comfortable being like me than like them. But it *can* cause problems.

One day the lieutenant called me into his office, closed the door and proceeded to tell me that the division had been contacted by the FBI who had been conducting an undercover sting operation to uncover police corruption within the department.

Keep in mind that police officers frequently work second jobs; most have families and they can't always make ends meet on what a cop makes. I was no different—over the years I've worked many second jobs. Particularly with a special needs child, when the insurance company won't cover the additional therapy and treatment Alex needed, we had to come up with the money somewhere, so I'd go get another job.

Many of my fellow officers were in the same boat. So they would find jobs suited to whatever skills they could offer in the marketplace. Several of them took jobs as sort of security guards protecting small, privately-owned clubs. This "security guard ring" was loosely organized by a handful of cops, and they would draw in their brother and sister cops with the promise of easy money, "just watching out for a few friends." Well, it turned out that these "clubs" were illicit gambling halls and the security guards were considered a form of illegal protection.

My heart sank as I listened. I knew what the next words out of his mouth would be, and sure enough, the next thing I heard was, "Chuck, I want you to go with the FBI guys and arrest these officers," and he handed me a list.

Dirty cops are, unfortunately, a fact of life. Given human nature, in any business, any profession or any industry, you'll find people who are greedy, stupid, psychologically warped or have some other unnamed reason for engaging in criminal activity. Police departments have their share; I'm not going to lie to you and say that cops are always above such behavior.

Cops are just people. Some strong, some weak. Some can't resist the temptation they see on the job. Walking into a room after busting a drug dealer and seeing $25,000 in tens and twenties lying on a table can seem like it's all the money in the world. *"It's drug money"*, a little voice whispers, *"who's gonna miss it? Who's gonna complain? The drug dealer?"*. Of course, the problem with that kind of thinking is that, inside somewhere, you have to know right from wrong, and you have to be able to look yourself in the mirror everyday and live with whatever you've done in your life. And some cops don't remember that.

So now my lieutenant is telling me I have to go arrest some of my fellow officers. These guys were men that I knew, had served with for years, some of them, knew from the department and police gatherings and parties outside. It made me sick to my stomach just thinking about it.

I respectfully told the lieutenant that I didn't think I was the right man for the job; not because I didn't think they'd done anything wrong, but because I'd fought and bled and made arrests with these guys. There were other officers with more distance on the situation, better able to handle it psychologically. The lieutenant overrode my objections and ordered me to go.

I obeyed, but I didn't like it. We arrested four officers that day. And I still recall it as one of my worst days on the force. I didn't sleep much that night.

Shortly after that, a lieutenant's position opened up (not the same one), and I took the civil service exam to see if I would qualify. I was still of the opinion that I could stay with the department and move up in the ranks and things would work out.

I've always done pretty well on tests, not because I'm brilliant or anything, but because I'm very methodical and study hard. So I take the civil service test, and got the highest score out of anyone in the department. I apply for the job and guess what happens? Another applicant who had close ties to the mayor's office was hired. This guy was universally disliked, had very little actual street work and so had very little credibility with the rank-and-file, but he had the political connections, so he got the job.

I was really pissed off. To be passed over for a well-deserved promotion hurts, no matter what profession you're in. And it's doubly aggravating when you know it's politically motivated. I'm a proponent of the "things happen for a reason" theory, but I had real problems with this development. I'd paid my dues, this guy hadn't. He only got the job on the basis of who he knew, not on his abilities or record of service. That kind of decision is hard to swallow.

The best thing I can say about this incident was that it was a true motivating factor in my life, because I really started concentrating on developing my real estate business. I had already begun investing in real estate and thought about it as a way to get off the force and start doing something else for a living, but at that point it wasn't an overwhelming, driving force in my life. If I *had* gotten the promotion, I might never have gotten into real estate to the extent that I did—I might have stayed with the department forever. So maybe that's why it happened, because it was certainly a tool that pried me away from police work.

So I began to view real estate as my ticket out. I didn't have any money but I *did* have good credit at that time; something that changed later on down the road, which I'll tell you about shortly. Real estate had always interested me. It seemed a great way to generate income and develop assets for my family. I figured I'd become a landlord: buy some properties; have a positive cash flow; the properties would increase in value every year; we'd be set for life. I started acquiring rental units, working long hours outside the department and building my real estate portfolio. And I was pretty successful at it. Finally, I felt I could see light at the end of the financial tunnel. It gave me hope that I could have a life after the department. And that was really important, because the internal politics were starting to drive me crazy.

We got a new Chief of Police right about then, and this guy was more than a political animal, he was a political hooker. Nothing was too far-fetched, too outlandish or too ridiculous if it would give him media exposure. He lived to see his name in bright lights, in the paper, on television. He was on a first-name basis with most of the media contacts in the city and he used his contacts to build his political career. I always thought that he would end up in state or local politics—he was that hungry for life in the limelight.

At any rate, one day I got called to a violent domestic incident. The initial report indicated a gun was possibly involved. I rolled to the scene and met another squad car there—with a gun involved you like to have several officers respond, for obvious reasons. We arrive at the house, and there's a lady, probably in her forties, standing just inside the door, screaming, terrified, trying to get away from this man standing just behind her with a shotgun. When he sees the police officers responding, he pushes her out the door and slams it behind her.

We take her to a safe position and attempt to find out what the problem is. This happened during the summer, when it's hot and muggy; it was probably 95 degrees that day. People always get more agitated when it's hot—you'd be amazed at how many more domestic violence calls we'd get during the summer months. The heat puts people on edge, and they're more likely to drink alcohol to cool themselves off, which only succeeds in releasing the stupidity hormones in their brain (not really, but I've always felt that was a true statement). At any rate, this lady proceeds to tell us there's also a young child in the house, who as far as she knows, is still inside. This would turn out later to be untrue—the child was smart enough to duck out the back door just about the time his mother was pushed out the front, but we didn't know that at the time.

As senior officer present, and not wanting to get any officers hurt, I called dispatch and asked for the SWAT team. Most of the SWAT team members carry their swat gear in their personal vehicles, so they can be ready at any time day or night to respond to a call. In most instances, swat members will be on scene within about thirty to forty-five minutes, an hour at most. While waiting for them to respond, I did all the things a scene commander should do: cordoned off the area; evacuated some of the nearby houses and called the hostage negotiator, who responded quickly. We also contacted the suspect's brother after his wife gave us his phone number, and he came over to the scene to add his assistance.

Three hours later, we're still waiting for the SWAT team. I called dispatch several times asking for the status, and was told they'd be on their way shortly. The media was already there; they listen to police scanners and roll on every call they find interesting, or feel will provide them with sound bites for the evening news. Part of scene control is keeping them well back from the scene, as well as neighborhood spectators, who all might be endangered if a suspect begins shooting.

Finally, the Police Chief shows up, followed by the SWAT team. The chief had contacted the SWAT team leader and ordered him to assemble the team at the station rather than responding to the scene so he could "lead the charge" out to collar this dangerous criminal holding the police at bay. It was surreal. He potentially endangered police officers and the suspect just so he could grab a little glory. Incredible. And there was more to come.

In the meantime, the hostage negotiator had done a good job in contacting the suspect and trying to talk him out of the corner he'd backed himself into. The suspect's brother also talked to him, and although they couldn't get him to come out of the house with his hands up, they did talk him into lying down on the living room floor and surrendering his weapon, which was a 12 gauge pump shotgun. SWAT moved in and disarmed him.

One of the basic rules of good police work is that you don't relax until the scene is safe; safe for officers, bystanders and anyone else in the vicinity. In a situation like this one, the SWAT commander is the one who determines when the scene is safe. The entire SWAT team needs to sweep the house, checking each room and possible hiding places to make sure there are no other suspects or danger to the officers.

Before I knew it, the Police Chief had come out from behind the barricades and motioned a film crew from a local TV station over to begin an interview on the front lawn of this house. Seeing this, the neighbors also began moving out from behind protection; kids started riding their bikes down the sidewalk; the media started crowding forward.

Thinking I had missed a radio call, I contacted the leader of the SWAT team who was still sweeping the house and asked him if all was clear. His answer: "Negative, negative. We're still sweeping." What would have happened if the SWAT team had found another suspect hiding in the house? And what if that suspect had come out with guns blazing? Can you imagine the media frenzy if someone had gotten killed? In his hurry to grab some glory for himself, that Chief not only potentially endangered police officers, but bystanders, kids, neighbors and media. It was truly unbelievable. I was so disgusted I wanted to walk over and punch him. I didn't, but I wanted to.

Another incident with the Chief involved an ex-partner of mine, who'd retired after being shot in the line of duty. He'd responded to a robbery, and the suspect shot him four times in the ensuing gun battle. After undergoing several surgeries and physical therapy, my partner eventually ended up retiring from the department, not surprisingly. This guy was sort of a political rabble-rouser. He loved to get on the mayor's case about political issues—he'd go to all the city council meetings and was very vocal about expressing his opinion to the council members. He was a real live wire, and the mayor couldn't stand him.

One day I get called into the Chief's office and told that I was assigned to go serve this ex-cop with a summons from the city: he was going to be brought up on charges of a housing code violation. Needless to say, I went ballistic. Here you have a guy that almost lost his life in defense of this city and now they're going to try prosecuting him on some trivial and trumped-up code violation? I refused to have anything to do with it. The Chief and I had words, some of which are frankly unprintable, and the end result was that I was suspended for three days for insubordination.

That didn't particularly bother me, because by that time I knew I was on my way out of the department, and I knew the Chief had it in for me. Besides, my real estate business was picking up nicely. In fact, during my suspension, I wholesaled a house and made about $6,000.00.

When I got back from my suspension, the Chief called me in to his office again to discuss the suspension. I think he was looking for an attitude problem on my part, and I wasn't going to give him the satisfaction. He gave me his number three speech: "I hope this won't affect our working relationship. I hope you don't have any hard feelings about this, blah, blah, blah." I responded simply, "No, Chief, no hard feelings, in fact I made $6,000 turning a real estate deal during the three days I was off, so no, there's no hard feelings at all." Somehow, I don't think my answer pleased him, because he turned beet-red and I thought his head was going to explode.

Sometimes the paybacks from superior officers had unexpectedly humorous results. There was a Lieutenant in the Detective's Bureau that I didn't see eye to eye with; in fact, we couldn't stand each other. Commanders have the authority to pull other officers off routine duty and designate them for a particular assignment. This lieutenant outranked me, and I was informed that the department had a special job for me. About this time, there was a certain area of the city that was one of the known hang-outs for prostitutes, and there had recently been several hookers that had been attacked and assaulted. Several of those prostitutes had actually been cross-dressers, and had been beaten up pretty severely. Nowadays, we'd probably call it a hate crime. Anyway, the department decided that someone needed to go undercover, someone that could handle themselves and react if they were targeted by whoever had been attacking the hookers. Guess who they picked to go undercover? Think I had made a few enemies during my time on the force? You bet.

Now, I have to tell you: at 6'1" and 240 pounds, I was the *ugliest* woman you've ever seen. How anyone could believe that I was a hooker was beyond me, but be that as it may, I dressed up and hung out on the corner. Can you believe this? No less than *five* guys stopped to solicit me. *Five guys!*

Were they blind? At any rate, I'm at the station a while later, and I walk through to booking, still dressed in my undercover finery, when I spot one of the guys who I'd arrested for solicitation. He looks at me and gets this sickened look on his face as he realizes just how ugly a woman I am. Shaking his head sadly, he says, "Damn, I gotta stop drinking!"

I was also the subject of several Internal Affairs Investigations. IA is a necessary part of any police organization—there are dirty cops and they need to be rooted out and drummed out of the department. Most rank-and-file officers despise IA investigators, not because of what they do, but because they do it with a holier-than-thou attitude and they see it as a way to make political hay. My problem with Internal Affairs is that I think they need to be a completely independent agency; not linked with the department in any way. It would add greatly to their credibility if they could function without consideration of the hierarchy within the department.

Being an honest cop, I never had anything to fear from IA investigations, and I think those that targeted me were undoubtedly generated by higher-ups that were frustrated by my non-political attitudes.

One investigation stemmed from a complaint filed by a lady whose son was arrested on an auto theft charge. He was a juvenile, and after he was released into her custody, she came back and said that the arresting officer had punched her son in the face in her presence. I was accused of using excessive force, and IA opened an inquiry. The investigating officer interviewed all the other police officers first, leaving me for last. He would inappropriately ask them leading questions about the incident instead of letting them tell what happened in their own words, but they were smarter than he was and described what happened accurately.

When it came time for my interview, I listened to his charges, and then pointed out very calmly that it was impossible for me to have done this, since I was *off duty at the time I was accused of punching this juvenile.*

I was home, not even at the station at that time. The IA officer's face fell, as he realized that he'd neglected to check basic facts of the case, and that he'd made a complete fool of himself.

Another time I came out of my house and saw an unmarked police car sitting down the block with two officers inside. Clearly, my house was under surveillance. I never could get IA to admit I was under investigation, but my real estate dealings were taking off. We had just moved into a new house in a nice neighborhood, and I figured they were trying to see if I had illegal funds coming in that were supporting my new lifestyle.

Kind of the final straw for me occurred when a local high school basketball star was murdered. This kid was, from all reports, going to be the next major player and NBA superstar; he was a good kid and amazingly talented. Unfortunately, he was in the wrong place at the wrong time, and got caught in a cross-fire between gang members. He wasn't in a gang; he was too smart for that, but he got killed nonetheless.

I was assigned the funeral detail by the watch commander, which was a little strange in itself. Ordinarily sergeants aren't assigned that kind of detail; patrol officers usually pull funerals. Maybe they figured it was going to be a large funeral, given the kid's status, and they wanted the community to know the police would be there to prevent any further trouble. At any rate, I was there in uniform and a marked police car; a definitive showing of police muscle.

It *was* a big funeral, with about two hundred mourners at the cemetery and, of course, a minister to lead the service. This kid was an important symbol in the African-American community, and they really turned out to support his family. So there I was, standing on the fringes of this service, and this white guy comes shuffling over to see what's going on. Turns out he had just been released from jail and was clearly disturbed; rambling and mumbling; dirty and a real loser by all appearances. He sees that a funeral is in progress and starts verbally harassing the mourners, yelling racial slurs and being really obnoxious. I went over and told him to stop, or I'd arrest him and take him in on charges. He started in on me, and got louder and more disruptive. I tried reasoning with him but he just wouldn't listen. Finally, with an inspired lack of common sense or wisdom, he took a swing at me. At that point, it's self-defense and he's trying to assault a police officer, so I popped him. One punch and he was down for the count. My backup showed up, and we put him in the back of the patrol car and took him away.

After the service, the minister came up to me and thanked me for taking care of this guy, and not allowing him to disrupt the ceremony any more than he had. I told the minister I might be hearing from the department, and would need him to make a statement about exactly what happened. The minister responded that if I needed it, all two hundred mourners would show up to testify on my behalf; an offer that surprised me with its generosity.

Sure enough, I got called in later to the watch commander's office, and told that an investigation would be opened into my use of excessive force on this guy. I knew they had no grounds for an inquiry, and at that point, I really didn't care if I burned bridges or not. I told the commander that if they filed charges against me, I would call two hundred people into his office that had been there, had seen the incident and would testify on my behalf. His face fell when he realized I was completely serious.

I never heard another word about the investigation, and about a month later, I retired from the force.

"Entrepreneurs are risk takers, willing to roll the dice with their money or their reputation on the line in support of an idea or enterprise. They willingly assume responsibility for the success or failure of a venture and are answerable for all its facets. The buck not only stops at their desk, it starts there too."
Victor Kiam

Chapter 4
My First Real Estate Experience

I'm a pretty decisive person. Once I make a decision to embark on a project, or take a course of action, I jump into it with all four feet, so to speak. And investing in real estate was a typical example. I just went about it the wrong way.

Don't get me wrong, I thought I'd done all my homework. I checked out other types of businesses; other ways of branching out and earning that additional money and security that I thought would benefit my family and I kept coming back to real estate. There are a million get-rich-quick, get-rich-slow, don't get-rich-at-all-but-think-you-will schemes out there; I think I looked at them all. And real estate seemed to hold the most promise.

I'd become a landlord, I decided. Well, we decided, actually: Amy and I. She recognized that police work was going to be the death of me sooner or later, whether by actual physical injury or stress overload, and she was anxious to see me out of that line of work.

Conventional wisdom at that time said you could buy "distressed" properties, fix them up and use them as rentals. Your tenants, by paying the rent, would also pay your mortgage payment on the property; and if you set things up the right way, you'd have a positive cash flow; meaning the rents you collected would be in excess of all the expenses for the rental: mortgage, insurance, repairs and anything else. Plus, the value of the rentals would increase every year, building equity that you could take out when you sold the property, or sooner if you wanted to refinance your mortgage. Simple and easy, right? In a perfect world, maybe, but the last time I looked, we don't live in a perfect world. Little did I realize what disasters were about to befall us.

But at that time, we thought we had a good plan. We had excellent credit at that time, and had a line of credit that we would use to assist us in purchasing our first rental. This was in 1995 and the housing market in and around Cleveland was full of "distressed" properties just begging for a buyer.

I now call these types of properties "junkers", because that's really what they are: cheap houses, usually in poor or blighted neighborhoods. If the owners ever lived in them, they didn't have the money to fix them up or pay for simple maintenance. These houses are usually in some state of disrepair: roofs leak, broken windows, water damage, tenant damage, things like that. Some major, some minor. Some cosmetic, some structural. You try to stay away from the ones with major damage, but sometimes you make an exception.

The advantage to buying junkers is that they're cheap— not just the construction, but the price. You can often buy them for fifty or sixty cents on the dollar. Many have been repossessed by the banks or mortgage companies that held the note on them; sometimes it's the owners that are one step ahead of the foreclosure paperwork and desperate to sell. Realtors often have a listing of junkers in their area— they'd rather sell you the "pretty" houses, but they won't pass up a chance to make a buck on a junker.

I was still working full time at the police department, and in my travels, I started checking out various neighborhoods and scoping out potential properties to buy. There was an amazing selection to choose from: the Cleveland metropolitan area in the mid-nineties seemed like it had more than its share of blighted areas. Union-Mills Park, Woodland Hills, Mt. Pleasant; all nice names for not-so-nice regions.

There's a big difference between buying distressed property, or fixer-uppers, and becoming a "slum landlord". Slum landlords have no interest in fixing up their run-down properties; they'll rent to anyone that can pay the rent. They'll ignore safety issues, refuse to make cosmetic repairs or even perform routine maintenance, like fresh paint or new carpet. They're not concerned about improving the property to increase the value of their holdings; appreciation is not a word in their vocabulary. They only want to know that there's enough bodies in the house or apartment or whatever to pay the mortgage payment and put money in their pocket. Nothing else. I wasn't about to become a member in the Slum Landlord's Association of America.

Fixer-uppers, on the other hand, can represent a real bargain for someone trying to get into real estate. Houses that are vacant, for example, may have been repossessed by the mortgage company or bank, which is understandably nervous about holding a property that they're not making money on. They might be willing to discount the sales price on that house just to generate revenue. Or homeowners that got in over their heads and couldn't make their mortgage payments, let alone do regular maintenance on their properties will be willing to sell just to avoid foreclosure. If you're handy with making repairs, or know a contractor who'll give you a good deal, fixer uppers make a lot of sense.

So I found this single family home, run down but livable, in a neighborhood that wasn't the best, but wasn't in the middle of a war zone, either. It was a foreclosure property, and the bank was anxious to have someone start making payments on it. Amy and I used our credit line to help qualify for the loan and went down and signed the paperwork, putting the house in our names. We were now the proud owners of our first rental. We had tenants in the house, the mortgage payment was covered, and it had a positive cash flow. Hey, this was pretty fun! Let's do it again!

I must admit I'm pretty adept at finding good deals. I'm an outgoing guy: I talk to people all day long, I'm interested in what they have to say, and I'm not shy about telling them what I do for a living, whether it's being a cop or investing in real estate. When I started telling people about being interested in buying rental properties, they started coming out of the woodwork.

If you're going to be successful in buying and holding rental properties, there are two things you need to become proficient in: estimating property repair costs and evaluating prospective tenants.

When you buy a pretty house, it's usually in a nice state of repair; the owner has usually lived in it and has a sense of pride in ownership, and tries to maintain the place in a reasonable fashion. You may have some painting to do, or landscaping, or other small things, but overall it's a nice house. That's why we call them pretty houses – because they are.

Distressed properties, or fixer-uppers, are by their definition in need of repair. You have to learn how to look at a property, do a thorough inspection, and determine if it's worth your while to bother with it. If you buy a property for $100,000, and it needs $20,000 worth of repairs, take a look at the market value of the repaired property. It the market value is only $120,000, it doesn't make a lot of sense to spend your time and money making the needed repairs. On the other hand, if the market value is $180,000, you'd be looking at a pretty good investment.

Your inspection should be comprehensive and very thorough. Take your time when doing an inspection, and take *lots* of notes. You can't possibly remember everything that needs to be done for each property you look at. You need to check out all aspects of the grounds, exterior and interior structures, systems and features. You're looking in all areas for items that will cost you money to fix. Obviously, big ticket items are less desirable than smaller, cosmetic repairs. The differences between re-grading and replacing a cracked concrete driveway and patching up some holes in interior sheetrock are enormous; thousands of dollars are at stake. Make sure you know what you're getting into.

Look at everything. Foundation to roof—are there obvious signs of damage that need to be addressed? If the house is settling off kilter, lower on one corner or one side than the other, that's an indication of foundation problems or structural issues. Porches and decks are one of the first places to deteriorate, and can cost big bucks to fix. Pools are problems from several aspects: they represent liability problems and the potential for accidents and astronomical repairs. Interior walls and ceilings: is there water damage? Plaster repair needed? Systems: plumbing, heating, air conditioning, sewer or septic—the list goes on and on.

You need to be able to check all these things, and have a good idea of what it will take to repair or replace each one. If you can't do the work yourself, you need a reliable contractor that won't charge you an arm and a leg to do the job. Over time, I got to be pretty good at evaluating repair costs on houses.

The other thing you need to get good at is finding reliable tenants. I'm not saying each one has to have perfect credit or been at their place of employment for 150 years, but you *do* want them to be able to pay the rent. A little "job jumping" is ok; it's more important that they work *consistently*, even if it's not always for the same employer. Check references; call their previous landlord and find out if they had any trouble with the tenant. Did they pay the rent on time? Eviction of a non-paying tenant can take a while—you need to know if they're dependable. If they're not, you'll end up making the mortgage payment out of your own pocket.

Do your homework. Don't always go with your gut instinct. A tenant may come across as perfectly reasonable and seem like a perfect candidate to rent your house, and later turn out to be the mother of all bad tenants. Trust me, I know.

But that wisdom came later. For now, Amy and I were pretty happy with the way things were shaping up. We had the house we lived in, the new (well, new to us) rental property that was bringing in money every month—I was still working full time for the department: things were definitely looking up. In fact, we were so encouraged by how the first rental unit worked out, we decided to go after more. And, boy, did we ever!

It didn't take long. Remember, at that point in my life, I still had good credit. Banks and mortgage companies were more than happy to let Amy and I sign loans and mortgages for more property. All of it in our own names. All of it income-producing. All rentals. Some came with tenants already renting the units, some tenants we had to find and screen.

Some needed more repairs than others; we'd do what work we could and contracted out the rest.

We went at it fairly aggressively: acquiring properties one right after another. It seemed for most of that year, we were at a bank or mortgage company or title office at least once a week. Within twelve months, we had built up a portfolio of forty-three rental properties. Single family homes, duplexes, town homes, even a rural place. More *than a million dollars in net worth: actual equity in the properties!* Man, we were sitting pretty. Or so we thought.

Then we got a notice we were being sued.

"I learned about the strength you can get from a close family life. I learned to keep going, even in bad times. I learned not to despair, even when my world was falling apart. I learned that there are no free lunches. And I learned the value of hard work."

Lee Iacocca

Chapter 5
The Decline and Fall of the Chuck Smith Empire

Boy, Shakespeare had it right. *The first thing we do, let's kill all the lawyers*, he wrote, and I can <u>really</u> identify with that. Not to condemn the entire legal profession; after all, they do have their uses, but there are lawyers who are a disgrace to the entire judicial system. Bottom feeders. Ambulance chasers. More intent on making a name for themselves than serving the best interest of their clients. Or taking on clients and filing lawsuits on their behalf that they know full well are based on trumped-up allegations. Not all are like that. But some are.

Don't misunderstand me. This is not just sour grapes because I had a horrendous experience with the legal system. This is, I believe, an honest assessment of some of the members of a profession that, if you're in the real estate investment business, you're going to have to deal with. You need to find one that you can work with, one that you can trust and one that is a true professional. They're out there, you just have to search hard to find the right one.

We live in a litigious society. Anyone can sue anyone else for almost any reason, and they frequently do. We've all seen examples of ridiculous lawsuits—people sue fast food chains because the food made them fat, or one of my personal favorites: a judge (yes, a *judge!*) in Germany sued Coca Cola because he drank two cokes every day for years and developed diabetes. So it must be Coca Cola's fault, right? Personal responsibility is at an all-time low. The real reason for this obnoxious behavior, of course, is the money. *The deeper the pockets you are perceived to have, the more likely you'll be named in a lawsuit.*

As a police officer I was, of course, intimately familiar with the justice system. I'd had my share of depositions and trials, attorneys and judges, and all the various and sundry proceedings and protocols that go along with it. There was nothing the legal system could show me that would surprise or scare me. Or so I thought.

When we received the official court summons that we were being sued, Amy and I were surprised, but not overly concerned. I mean, we knew we would have to defend ourselves, but at no time did we ever have an inkling of the scope of the disaster that was about to befall us.

The suit came from one of our tenants who lived in one of our two-story rentals. She had apparently unlocked an upper window, plus the protective screen outside, and her toddler had crawled through the unlocked window and screen and fallen to the porch below. Why she had unlocked the window and screen I have no idea; I never did receive an explanation that made any sense. And, in truth, it really didn't matter, because, as I said, personal responsibility is at an all-time low in our society. What really mattered was that the baby was injured, not seriously, but the tenant ran out and retained an attorney.

I don't want to appear unsympathetic; I have kids that I adore, and I'd hate to see any of them get hurt. And accidents can happen to anyone. But I also believe strongly in parental responsibility. If a baby gets locked inside a car on a hot day and dies of heat stroke, is that an accident, or parental neglect?

At any rate, this attorney did some investigation, and soon found that Amy and I owned a great deal of real estate. It wasn't hard to discover, as all the real estate was in our names. I'm sure her attorney heard the *ka-ching* of a big payday when he realized we had assets that he could go after. No doubt his eyes lit up and he started licking his lips in anticipation of a large contingency fee.

I have to tell you: I've been sued more as a real estate investor than as a police officer, which is kind of surprising. But, as I indicated, it's the *perception* of wealth that makes people want to come help themselves to a piece of it, and people don't perceive cops as having wealth. Which is pretty much true in most cases.

This was at the end of our first year as real estate investors, and although Amy and I had amassed a small fortune in property, I was still working full-time at the police department. We'd moved into a larger house during this year, but our lifestyle really hadn't changed all that much. I was still working too many hours, and although the money situation had gotten better, we still had a lot of medical and therapy expenses for our autistic son that ate up a lot of the profits from our rentals.

We knew absolutely nothing about asset protection at that point. I had never even heard the *concept* of protecting your assets, let alone done anything about it. That old adage about *if I'd know then what I know now* really applies here. You see, if someone sues you and gets a judgment against you, <u>they can come after anything you own in your own name.</u> Everything you have is at risk.

And as a real estate investor, you can be sued by such a wide variety of people: tenants, other Realtors, contractors, sellers, buyers, partners, the general public, etc., etc., etc. Sometimes you feel you're walking around with a target painted on your back, or a sign that simply says "Sue me". I'm not trying to scare you; I'm just trying to get across to you how important asset protection is. Once you have a full and complete understanding of how to protect your assets, you can not only become wealthy, you can **remain** wealthy, which is just as important as accruing the assets in the first place.

So there we are: Amy and I, fat, dumb and happy, so to speak, thinking that we'd provided well for our family and given them a measure of security. Nothing could have been further from the truth, but we were completely unaware of that. The lawsuit disturbed us, of course, but we had faith in the system, and didn't really understand the chain of events that had been set in motion by the suit.

We went through all the standard protocols of a legal proceeding: depositions, investigators, doctors reports, and still felt that we would come out ok. Then the bombshell—the tenant received a huge judgment against us: almost *half a million dollars!* We were thunderstruck. How could this have happened?

All of a sudden, I'm lying awake at night wondering how this is going to affect my family, our properties, our lives. How are we going to pay for this judgment? Could we possibly settle with the tenant and her attorney?

I actually sold a couple of our rentals, and tried to talk the attorney into settling for a lesser amount than the judgment, but he had those dollar signs in his eyes, and wouldn't seriously consider it. I have to tell you: this guy was the type of attorney who really doesn't have the best interest of his client at heart, because he ultimately ended up collecting less than the amount of the settlement I offered him; so who received less in their pocket at the end of the process? His client. But that apparently wasn't as important to him as trying to ruin my life, which he nearly succeeded in doing.

It soon became apparent that he was going to pick off our properties one by one, forcing a sale in each case and attaching the profits as each was sold. He even tried to come after my wages from the police department, and that's where I drew the line. These people have absolutely no regard for the effect that they have on your life. It's not even a consideration when they're calculating how they can collect on what you have. A wife and kids? Who cares? They'll attach your wages and force you to sell your property without a backward glance for the time and effort and sweat you put into building it up. Put your family out on the street? Sure, if they can. Don't think for a minute that they care what happens to you and yours. They don't.

This period was an incredibly stressful time in our lives, as you can imagine. To have worked as long and hard as we did to accumulate what wealth we had, only to watch it start down the drain was not only heart-breaking but humbling. We had been living the American dream, and now that dream was shattered. Amy and I hung in there somehow; I'm not sure how. Our marriage stood up under the pressure, but we spent plenty of nights agonizing over the decisions we had made and the direction we should take for the future.

There's a story that's told about Mrs. Charlton Heston; the lady's who's been married to Moses, Ben Hur and a great many other memorable characters over her husband's decades-long acting career. Anyway, an interviewer asked her if she had ever considered divorcing her famous husband. After a long and thoughtful pause, she reportedly said: "Divorce, no. Murder, yes."

I'm sure Amy felt the same way about me. Especially during this time.

We got some legal advice of our own, and were told the only way we could save even a remnant of what we had was to file bankruptcy. Chapter 7 bankruptcy, a full-on complete financial surrender. All the good credit we had worked so hard to achieve, ruined. All the rentals, which were being picked off one by one. We would be left with the home we lived in, our personal belongings and our cars. Nothing else.

The house of cards had come tumbling down around our ears. It was a bitter and humiliating decision, but we had no other choice. We had to cut our losses to save what we could.

What in the hell was I going to do now?

Chapter 6
My Second Real Estate Experience
(Quite a Difference!)

I had to do *something*. I couldn't just take this defeat lying down. I had worked too hard to build up something for my family to hold onto, to just watch it get torpedoed by some low-life. There had to be a way to rebuild my life. They say that *whatever doesn't kill you makes you stronger*. I made a vow to myself right then and there that this wasn't going to kill me. Life is all about choices. The choice I made at that moment in my life was one I would never regret. *Never give up*. If you do, they might as well call the undertaker for you, because you might as well be dead.

Strangely enough, I *still* had faith in real estate. I still had a gut feeling that real estate would be my saving grace. Don't ask me why. Certainly Amy didn't share my feeling—at that point "real estate" was a four-letter word to her. And I can't say that I blamed her.

I was still working at the department on a full-time basis, but I started looking around at different real estate seminars and courses and what they called "boot camps" being held around the Cleveland area. Now, this is just my personal opinion, but after looking at the wide variety of these types of seminars that are being offered, I've got to say that the vast majority of them are crap. Pure, unadulterated crap. The people putting them on are making money off of the products that they sell at these courses: books, videos, things like

45

that. Most of them never put their money where their mouths are; they've never actually put into practice what they're preaching to you. It's a case of "do as I say, not as I do." And when the system they're selling doesn't work for you, they'll point the finger at you and say, "well, it's *your* fault, it's not *my* system."

At any rate, I happened to run into a guy by the name of Ron LeGrand at one of these seminars—he happened to be in Cleveland making what amounted to a sales presentation for one of his boot camps, and my father and I went to listen to him. I was really surprised; what he said made a lot of sense to me.

Ron talked about how he had gotten started in the real estate business as a landlord, and even though he'd built up a lot of property value and was very successful, the way he had gotten into it wasn't the way to go. He held property in his own name, and in the beginning didn't know anything about asset protection. Does this sound familiar? He might have taken the script for my life and been speaking from it. Because it was so familiar, because I felt like he was speaking directly to me, I listened. I listened very carefully. And I realized I wasn't the only one who had made that mistake. This guy had been where I was. Or pretty close.

I wanted to hear more. I wanted to attend his boot camp. I wanted to purchase his home study course. And I couldn't afford any of it. Keep in mind that my bankruptcy had just been discharged maybe a month before I went to this seminar. I'd had to give up all my credit cards when I filed the bankruptcy, and my credit was shot. In fact, just going to the seminar had created some waves at home, because Amy was sick to death of hearing about real estate. She'd been down that path already, and it wasn't to her liking. She didn't want to hear that her husband wanted to spend money learning how to get involved in real estate "the right way" this time. So there I was, like a kid in a candy shop with no pennies in his pocket, looking at the rows and rows of sweets. Lucky for me my dad was with me that day.

The price of a good education is never cheap. Whether you go to Harvard or simply the School of Hard Knocks, it's gonna cost you.

Ron LeGrand's home study course cost several thousand dollars. I didn't have it. My dad looked at me, looked at the material spread out in front of us, and never hesitated for a minute. Out came the plastic; he charged the whole thing to his credit card, and we were off. Sometimes, those closest to you have more faith in you than you have in yourself, especially at a low point in your life. Like I said, lucky my dad was with me that day.

I took that home study course, and started reading. It came with audio tapes, and I'd take the whole package with me when I went to work and listen to the tapes on a little hand-held audio cassette recorder. I was working the night shift with the department then, and I was a Sergeant, so I didn't have a partner to worry about disturbing. I'd study the manual on my breaks—I think I must have studied almost non-stop for a little more than three weeks.

Ron LeGrand was one of the top guys in the country when it came to quick turning houses, and so much of what he said I could apply to my own situation. Within about 30 days of buying the home study course and, well, studying my brains out, I turned my first real estate deal using Ron's system. And netted about $25,000.00.

Yep, that's right. Twenty five grand. On one sale. I brought my first real estate check home and handed it to my wife. "Here, honey, use this for whatever you want. There'll be plenty more where that came from." I knew she wouldn't do anything crazy with it, like run out and buy an expensive car or designer clothes; it just felt so good to be able to hand her a check for that amount and watch her face, and know that there *would* be more where that came from. I felt vindicated, and once more confident that I could provide for my family in the way I wanted.

I want to talk for a minute about continuing education. I said earlier that the price of a good education is never cheap, and that's really true. In the years since I had to file bankruptcy, I've spent countless hours attending seminars, classes, boot camps and anything else that would further my education and knowledge of real estate and business in general. I put aside a certain percentage of my profits for educational expenses. For me. As this is being written, I've probably spent in excess of $70,000.00 on different forms of education and training. I look at it as investing in myself; in my future. I made serious mistakes once, due to lack of knowledge and schooling, and it had serious consequences in my life, and the lives of my family. I don't ever want to make that mistake again. Knowledge truly *is* power.

You have to make personal development a priority in your life. I mean a *top* priority. You'll run across people who I call the "dream stealers". For whatever reason, sometimes even subconsciously, those around you will sabotage your efforts to better yourself and succeed in life. Sometimes they do it out of fear; fear that you'll succeed where they've failed, or fear that you'll leave them if you succeed. Sometimes it's a co-dependency thing, where they need you to act a certain way so they can act a certain way. Whatever the reason, they'll tell you "you can't" do something, or react in a negative way to any new idea you propose, or shoot down your ambitions. In effect what they're doing is stealing your dreams, because after a steady diet of that kind of demoralizing, you'll give up on those dreams, and they'll be gone. *You're the only one that can stop that from happening.* Don't ever give up on yourself, or your dreams. It's your responsibility; no one else's. Take control of your own destiny. Don't listen to the naysayers.

So, anyway, I started going to seminars and classes of all sorts. Some of them, like I said, weren't worth the money. But I gleaned what I could from them, and went on to the next one. Some of them had more value, and I used that to build on what I knew. This whole time I was starting to rebuild the wealth I had lost in my first go-around with real estate, and I would write down what worked for me, and *what didn't work.* I would learn a point here or there in the seminars I was attending, and I'd work that into the mix. If something made sense, I'd try it. If it didn't work, I'd toss it. If it worked, I'd incorporate it. And I wrote all this down, which eventually became the basis for my own real estate course. But we'll get to that shortly.

Around this time I met another man who would become a mentor to me: John Ulmer of Toledo, Ohio. John was another top name in real estate investing, and I learned a lot from him.

Each system I looked at had its own set of gaps and holes; some were more complete than others, but still lacking what I felt was a total package. No one offered what I thought was a complete and comprehensive system that would give the new real estate investor a real shot, right out of the gate, at financial success. The more systems I looked at, the more convinced I was. There was a real need here for someone to put all the pieces together in a coherent, cohesive fashion.

My first year in the business of quick-turning houses I made $150,000.00. Cash in hand. Working part time. Don't forget I was still with the police department, working a forty-plus hour work week. I would then work my real estate business after I'd put in my eight or nine hour shift at the department. And when I say I was working it part time, I mean really part time – maybe eight to ten hours a week.

Almost the entire focus of my real estate business that first year was in wholesaling. That's where you buy a house for a deeply discounted price, and sell it for a markup to another real estate investor, either to a landlord-type who's planning on renovating or fixing it up and using it as a rental, or to an investor who's going to fix it up and re-sell it quickly. I did very little retailing that first year, which usually entails buying a property, renovating it, then selling it to an owner-occupant who plans on living in the property, rather than using it as a rental.

I also did quite a bit of contract assignments, which is simply buying a property and turning over your position in that property quickly and for a small contract price – in my case it was a pre-determined fee, somewhere between fifteen hundred and three thousand dollars. Contract assignments required very little of my time or effort, so they were a nice little profit center for me.

I ran my real estate business out of an eight-by-ten office in my home, for a number of years. Doing the kind of real estate that I do, you really don't require a fancy office in a downtown location, with big windows and an expensive lease and people up front greeting potential clients. That's all ego-stroking stuff that is completely unnecessary. You don't need it. What people are interested in is results; not fancy window-dressing.

At any rate, my business started to grow. And people started to notice. Other investors started coming to me, asking if I could train them and show them how I did what I did. Although I enjoyed teaching—I taught at the Police Academy level on several occasions—I didn't feel I really was ready to teach real estate to other investors yet. Let me get a few more successful seasons under my belt. But when people want to learn something, and they feel you can teach them, they don't give up. They're insistent. And soon I had people coming to me offering me three thousand dollars a day, if I would just let them hang out with me and show them the basics of what I did.

Was I on to something here? Or were they? Maybe I *did* have something to offer in the arena of real estate investing. So I started designing my own course.

*"Man must cease attributing his problems to his environment,
and learn to exercise his will – his personal responsibility."*
Albert Schweitzer

Chapter 7
Stories From Some of My Real Estate Deals
(with copies of checks)

I think it's time I proved to you that I'm for real. That I'm not just blowing smoke, that the system that I'm talking about, the boot camps and seminars and one-on-one coaching sessions really do work.

Like I've told you, I've been to countless seminars and boot camps put on by others, and the vast majority of them are crap. Sometimes the people putting on the seminars will include success stories from their students, but it's interesting to note that they almost *never* include their own success stories. Why?   Because they don't make their money using their own systems; they make their money selling you things: books, tapes, seminars, things like that. *But they're not out there putting their financial future and the security of their families on the line day after day.* They want you to do that, but they won't do it themselves. What does that tell you about their motives?

It tells you that they're simply salesmen (or women), and all they're really interested in is selling you a product. If you go out and make a success of yourself, so much the better; they can use your story as an example of how good they are and how terrific their system is. But they're not really interested in seeing you succeed.

I, on the other hand, have the ultimate goal of doing everything I can to make sure that you succeed using my system. I did it, and if *I* can do it, *you* can do it. This is how I made my money, turned my life around from disaster and despair, and rose to the top again. You can do the same thing.

I work on average 25-30 hours a week, and typically make between $850,000 and a $1,000,000 a year using my own system. That's not selling you boot camps and seminars. *That's using my own system of quick-turning houses for instant cash.* My family depends on that income. Our financial future is wrapped up in what I do. I'm putting my money where my mouth is, because I'm actually practicing what I'm preaching to you.

My system is the most complete, effective, realistic and profit-generating real estate system available, bar none. This includes all the systems sold by those people who have mentored me. What I cover in this system works in the real world. I know that for a fact, because I use it on a daily basis. I only teach a very few seminars and boot camps a year – other than that, I'm out there doing real estate deals every single day.

I'm not trying to sell you numerous products, or enroll you in each new seminar or boot camp; my system covers every thing you need in a single source. In all of my training materials, you'll see actual examples of *my own* marketing successes, not just that of my students.

But let me show you some of those examples:

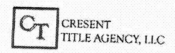

**CRESENT
TITLE AGENCY, LLC**

June 6, 2003

To Whom this May Concern:

Please be advised that I, Jeffrey D. Haines, Esq., am a Principal and General Counsel for Cresent Title Agency, LLC.. That I have personal knowledge of the facts to which this letter addresses and further attest to the validity of this writing.

That I have had an ongoing business relationship with Chuck Smith over the past five (5) plus years. That during this time, numerous checks have been drafted to either himself or his company from our escrow account as the direct result of the closing of a real estate transaction. That all of the checks that are represented throughout his course materials are valid copies or the actual checks drafted from Cresent Title Agency, LLC.

Sincerely,

JEFFREY D. HAINES, ESQ.
General Counsel / Principal

JDH/hh

Before me, a Notary Public for and in the state of Ohio, personally came Jeffrey D. Haines, who signed his name to this document this _6_ day of June, 2003, as his free act and deed.

_____
Notary Public

PHYLLIS COSTINEZO, Notary Public
State of Ohio
My Commission Expires April 2, 2007

4914 Hills & Dales Road
Canton, Ohio 44708
Phone: (330) 477-3299   Fax: (330) 477-3256
1-866-506-3591   ctb@cresenttitle.com

*Sworn Affidavit attesting to the validity of the checks
you'll see in this book.*

Here are copies of actual checks I have received for real estate deals I have been involved in (and the stories behind them):

CRESENT TITLE AGENCY, LLC
ESCROW ACCOUNT
59106
LOAN CLOSING/DATTILO
--Six Thousand Six Hundred Forty Two and 00/100 Dollars
June 6, 2003
$ *****6,642.00
PAY TO THE ORDER OF MONTEREY INVESTMENTS, INC.

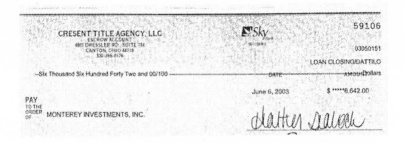

Figure 7-1
This was a wholesale deal – I owned the property 3 days.
This check represents my net profit.

T-TITLE AGENCY, INC.
ESCROW ACCOUNT
KEYBANK NATIONAL ASSOCIATION
894(
Proceeds to Seller
--Six Thousand Two Hundred Sixty Four and 64/100 Dollars
DATE January 3, 2002
AMOUNT $ *****6,264.64
TO THE ORDER OF Monterey Investments, Inc.

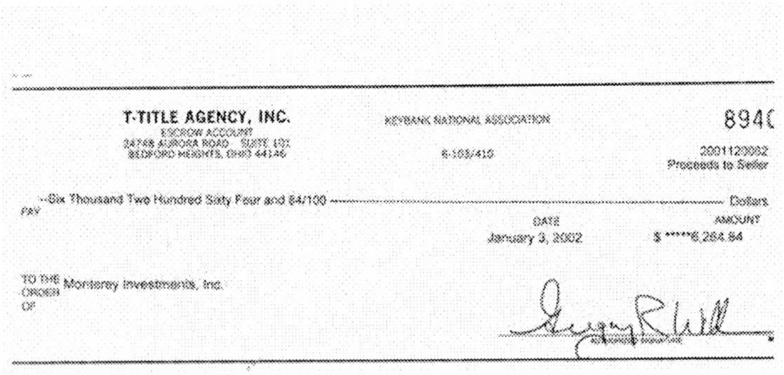

Figure 7-2
This was a wholesale deal. I owned the property two weeks.

Chuck Smith

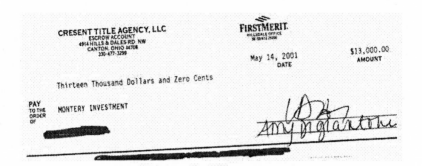

Figure 7-3
This was a wholesale deal I owned for one day!

Figure 7-4
This was a wholesale deal I owned for 5 days

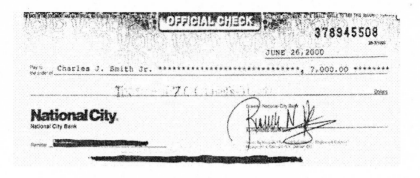

Figure 7-5
A wholesale deal I owned for one hour!

Figure 7-6
Wholesale deal. Owned 9 days.

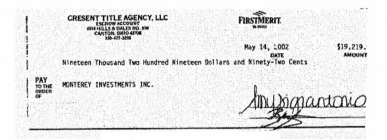

Figure 7-7
My largest wholesale deal to date. Owned property 1 week.

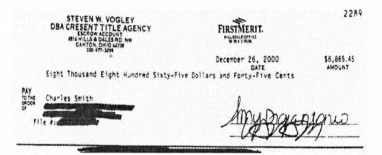

Figure 7-8
Wholesale deal. Owned 6 days.

Here's one for a four unit building:

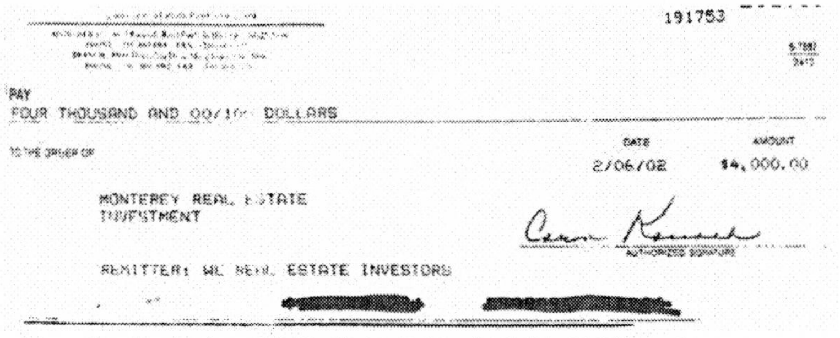

Figure 7-9
Seller paid me $4,000.00, then I turned around and sold the deed for
$10,000.00:

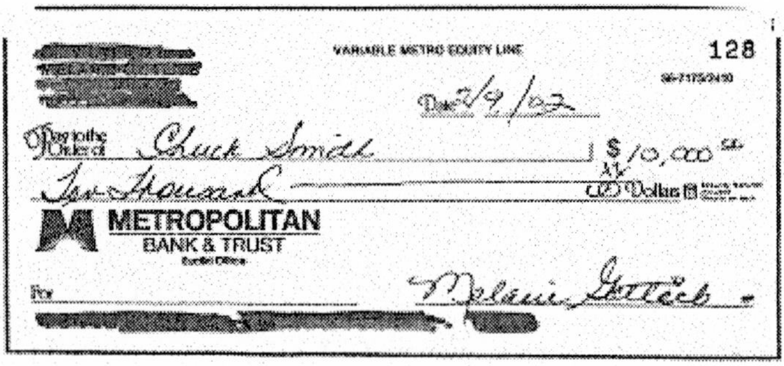

Figure 7-10
Total profit on this property $14,000.00

Figure 7-11
This was a wholesale deal I owned 10 days.

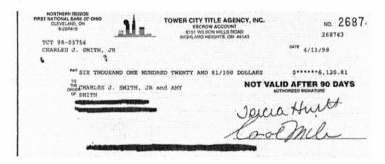

Figure 7-12
This was a wholesale deal. I owned this house 10 days.

Figure 7-13
This was a wholesale deal. I owned the house 4 days.

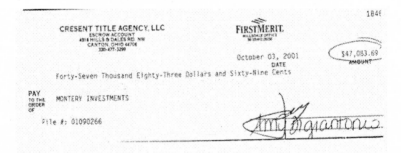

Figure 7-14
This was a deal that involved 100% owner financing. I originally expected
to make only $32,000 on this deal, but then I got the owner to discount
the mortgage by another $15,000, which resulted in an additional
$15,000 profit.

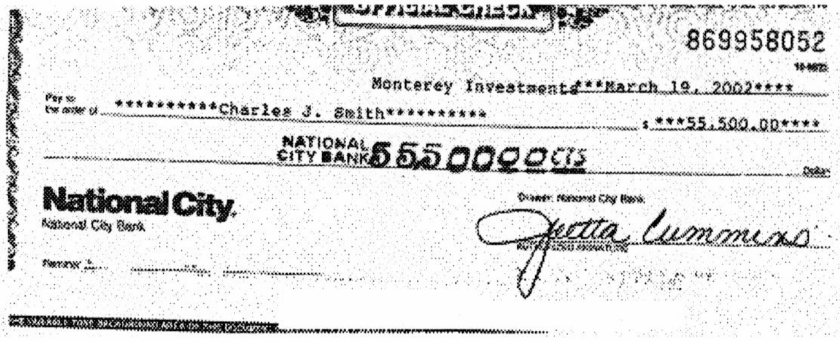

Figure 7-15
This is a retail deal on a high-end house.
The checks are bigger, but it's usually a one-time deal.

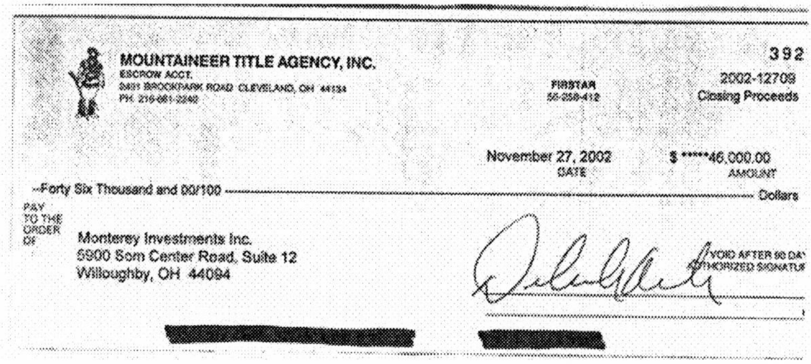

Figure 7-16
This is another retail deal on a high-end house.

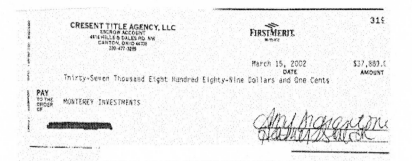

Figure 7-17
This is another retail deal on a high-end house.

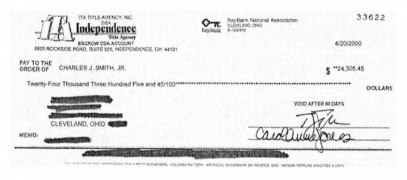

Figure 7-18
This was a retail deal to a landlord. I owned this property 4 weeks.

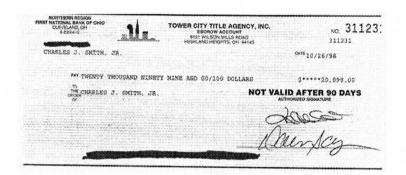

Figure 7-19
This is another deal to a landlord. I owned this one 3 weeks.

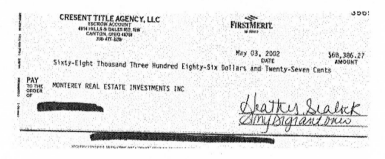

Figure 7-20
This was a retail deal on a high-end house.
To date, this has been my largest profit on a single transaction.
I owned this house 7 weeks.

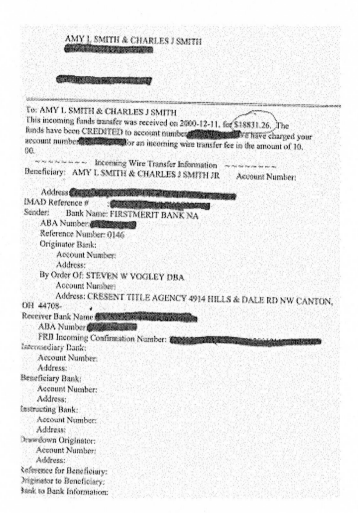

AMY L SMITH & CHARLES J SMITH

To: AMY L. SMITH & CHARLES J SMITH
This incoming funds transfer was received on 2000-12-11, for $18831.26. The
funds have been CREDITED to account number ⬛⬛⬛⬛ We have charged your
account number ⬛⬛⬛⬛ for an incoming wire transfer fee in the amount of 10.
00.

~ ~ ~ ~ ~ ~ ~ ~ Incoming Wire Transfer Information ~ ~ ~ ~ ~ ~ ~ ~
Beneficiary: AMY L SMITH & CHARLES J SMITH JR   Account Number:

    Address: ⬛⬛⬛⬛⬛⬛⬛⬛⬛
IMAD Reference #   ⬛⬛⬛⬛⬛⬛
Sender: Bank Name: FIRSTMERIT BANK NA
    ABA Number: ⬛⬛⬛⬛
    Reference Number: 0146
    Originator Bank:
        Account Number:
        Address:
    By Order Of: STEVEN W VOGLEY DBA
        Account Number:
        Address: CRESENT TITLE AGENCY 4914 HILLS & DALE RD NW CANTON,
OH 44708-
Receiver Bank Name ⬛⬛⬛⬛⬛⬛
    ABA Number ⬛⬛⬛⬛
    FRB Incoming Confirmation Number: ⬛⬛⬛⬛⬛⬛⬛⬛
Intermediary Bank:
    Account Number:
    Address:
Beneficiary Bank:
    Account Number:
    Address:
Instructing Bank:
    Account Number:
    Address:
Drawdown Originator:
    Account Number:
    Address:
Reference for Beneficiary:
Originator to Beneficiary:
Bank to Bank Information:

Figure 7-21
This was one of two deals I concluded at the airport as
Amy and I were leaving for the Bahamas.

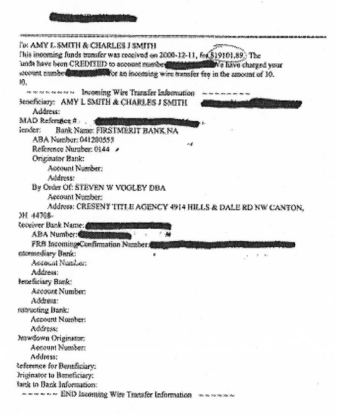

AMY L SMITH & CHARLES J SMITH

To: AMY L SMITH & CHARLES J SMITH
This incoming funds transfer was received on 2000-12-11, for $19101.89. The
funds have been CREDITED to account number ▓▓▓▓ We have charged your
account number ▓▓▓▓ for an incoming wire transfer fee in the amount of 10.
00.

~~~~~~~~~ Incoming Wire Transfer Information ~~~~~~~~~
Beneficiary: AMY L SMITH & CHARLES J SMITH
Address:
MAD Reference # :
Sender: Bank Name: FIRSTMERIT BANK NA
ABA Number: 041200553
Reference Number: 0144
Originator Bank:
Account Number:
Address:
By Order Of: STEVEN W VOGLEY DBA
Account Number:
Address: CRESENT TITLE AGENCY 4914 HILLS & DALE RD NW CANTON,
OH 44708-
Receiver Bank Name:
ABA Number:
FRB IncomingConfirmation Number:
Intermediary Bank:
Account Number:
Address:
Beneficiary Bank:
Account Number:
Address:
Instructing Bank:
Account Number:
Address:
Drawdown Originator:
Account Number:
Address:
Reference for Beneficiary:
Originator to Beneficiary:
Bank to Bank Information:
~~~~~~~~ END Incoming Wire Transfer Information ~~~~~~~~

Figure 7-22
This is the other deal I concluded at the airport before
heading for the Bahamas.

So why did I feel it necessary to show you copies of checks I've received? Because there's nothing like proof in black and white to show you that I'm for real. I don't just talk the talk; I walk the walk.

And when you see for yourself just how lucrative this business can be, you'll get as excited as I am about it!

"At the end of the day, it does not matter how many employees you have, what your gross profit was, how many deals you have done, how busy you were, how many houses you looked at, how many houses you bought, how many houses you sold, how many people who know who you are, you're the biggest, you're the best. No, the only thing that matters is: how much of a net profit did you make, and what must you do to consistently repeat it?"
Chuck Smith

Chapter 8
Overview of My Real Estate System

When I first started thinking seriously about designing my own course to teach people how to succeed in the real estate business, I knew I wanted to offer something completely different from what was already on the market. I didn't want a product that was all hype, all screaming banner headlines and marketing tricks. I wanted to offer a solid, no-nonsense course that people could put to use right away, and turn their lives around the way I had. I wanted a product I could be pleased with; one that I'd be proud to have my name on.

I'm a straight-ahead kind of guy, and the seminar I envisioned would reflect that quality: up-front, full of good information and common sense. I'd been taking notes and gathering information from all the other seminars I'd been attending over the years, trying new approaches and techniques I'd learned from others; keeping what worked and throwing out what didn't. As I accumulated more information and gained more direct, hands-on experience, I found my volume of notes got thicker and thicker as time progressed. Every time I sold another house and took another check home to my wife, I'd record what was effective, and what clearly didn't work. All these notes, all that experience, became the basis for my course – "Quick Cash Ultimate Real Estate Investment System ™". It's everything I've learned about this business, distilled into one easy-to-understand course.

Now, I'm not tooting my own horn here; well, ok, maybe I am, but parts of my course are so different from the other courses out there, and so effective, that I've had certain features of my system trademarked and registered with the U.S. Patents Office. That's an unusual step, but it gives you an idea of how good my program is. Let me give you a brief overview of the course, then I'm going to talk about one of the parts that I've had trademarked.

There are two important points to remember about being in business:

The real reason for being in business is for *the business to support you,* not *for you to support the business.* It is not our responsibility to employ people.

A real business is something you *take money out of*, not put money into or be held captive by.

It's amazing to me how many people either never learned those two things, or have long since forgotten them.

Overview of My System

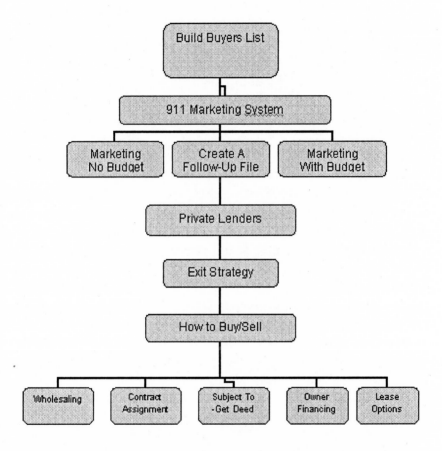

This is an overview of what you need to do to run a successful real estate investment business.

Every step you take using my system is a pre-planned, common sense approach to real estate investing. It's so straightforward and logical; you'll wonder why all the other so-called "gurus" out there didn't think of it themselves. Maybe because it's like I said, they're more interested in selling you products than putting their money where their mouth is, and actually doing real estate deals. This is not rocket science, folks. All it takes is a roadmap, and some determination. I give you the roadmap. The determination is up to you.

Building and Cultivating a Buyers List®

The very first step of my system is to Build and Cultivate a Buyers List®. I can't stress the importance of this enough. While I was still working full-time as a police officer, I managed to wholesale no less than five houses per month with an average profit of $10,000 each. My average customer, or buyer, purchases not one but *five* houses from me during the course of our business relationship! Experts in the field are stunned at how much profit I was able to generate. And the reason I was able to accomplish this was that I continuously build and cultivate a buyer's list®. In fact, this is one of the parts of my system that I've had trademarked.

I've traveled all over the country, attending seminars, teaching seminars and speaking with everyone I can who's involved in the real estate field; it never ceases to amaze me that this topic is rarely discussed. Except by me.

If your intention is to become a successful real estate investor, you must first build your foundation out of granite, not shaky sand. Now, I realize that this view isn't shared by many of the so-called "experts" in the field; they'll tell you,

"Oh, just run out and buy properties, and run ads in the paper. You'll find buyers."

In my opinion, that's a mistake.

I teach all of my students: the very *first* thing you do is Build and Cultivate a Buyers List®. Before you advertise, before you run out and start making offers on properties, *before you do anything else*, build a buyers list.

There are three main reasons for Building and Cultivating a Buyers List®:

1. It determines in what area(s) of town where the greatest demand is, and where you should be focusing your energy. For example, in the city where I do business, Cleveland, Ohio, if several buyers want houses on the southeast side of town, that's where my marketing will be targeted. I'll have my Realtors bring me listings from that area. That's where my street signs will go, and my billboards. It's the law of Supply and Demand. If there's a demand for properties on the southeast side, I become the supplier.

2. It ensures your houses will be quickly sold. What good does it do you to get a great deal on a property if no one wants to buy it from you? That's Basic Market Research 101, if you ask me. It is extremely rare that I sit on a house more than a few weeks. When I make a deal on a property, I already have several buyers in mind. I had one real estate "guru" tell me that my credibility would be ruined if I attracted buyers and didn't have a house to sell them. If that were true, I would have been out of business a long time ago, because it's rare that I ever have inventory. I'm very honest with my buyers; I tell them up

front I have no houses. Contrary to conventional wisdom, it actually whets their appetite and makes them hungry, motivated buyers who are anxious to do business with me, even if it means they have to wait for me to find them an appropriate property.

3. Having a buyers list keeps the cash flow machine running. Even if you have a great real estate machine going, you may be forced to slow down or even stop buying properties in the event the selling side of your business hits a snag. Our business is really no different from any other business; the houses we buy are the inventory we hold, and everyone knows that excess inventory that isn't being sold is a killer for any business.

There are a variety of ways to build a buyers list. My course gives many more options and methods, but here are a couple that work well:

! **Run an ad in the newspaper**

If you open up any newspaper in any major city, you'll see certain types of ads. The problem with most of these ads is that they're old and overused. In addition, these ads are designed to attract cash only buyers who want fixer upper properties. When I run an ad, I want to attract as many types of buyers as possible. I also want to attract buyers who have the ability to pre-screen themselves out of the process. Following is one of many ads included in my course, and it will make your phone ring off the hook with quality buyers:

"Investor relocating – has 17 properties, single/multi-family. Must sell. No money down. Must have good credit. Possible cash-out at closing. Serious buyers only. Free 25" color TV with purchase. Call XXX-XXX-XXXX."

Now, you don't really have to be relocating, just considering it. Every winter in Cleveland I *consider* moving to Florida, but I never actually *do* it. When you use this ad, you don't have to specifically mention cash buyers, because they'll call anyway.

! Real Estate Investment Clubs

The monthly meetings for these clubs are filled with people who want to buy properties for investment, but are afraid to. They really want someone to "hold their hand" and show them the way. By becoming a "Counselor-Seller"™, determining what exactly it is they want, and providing support, you can become very wealthy off of this segment of real estate investors. These people are looking to build a rental portfolio, and by catering to them, you can reap handsome rewards.

My goal is to always find houses for a buyer, not to find buyers for a house. That's an important distinction, and it's been wildly successful. I have been personally responsible for more investors being successful in my area that anyone else. I make money and my buyers call me for advice and counseling. It's a win/win situation all around.

There are three basic types of buyers:

1. Owner-occupants

Just what it sounds like – they own the house they're living in. You'll make your largest profit on these buyers per deal, but it's usually a one-shot opportunity.

2. Investor/Rehabbers
    They buy houses, renovate or repair them, and sell them. They need you, because without houses, they can't make money.

3. Investor/Landlords
    You'll make the easiest and most money with these buyers. They are interested in cash flow and long-term appreciation, not a quick buck. I cater to these buyers. As a Counselor-Seller, I accommodate them in every way possible. If they want a property rehabbed while there are tenants already in there paying the rent, that's fine with me. I'll do everything I can to make that deal happen. But believe me, I get well compensated for my efforts. It's much easier to sell 5 houses to a single buyer, than 5 houses to 5 different buyers. So I cultivate this type of buyer; I regularly take these buyers out to dinner at expensive restaurants, or take them to sporting events. I even took two of my best customers on a cruise. Basic Sales 101 says take care of your customers, and they'll take care of you.

A final point I want to make about buyers concerns what I call the "buyer's impulse window." This is the point where a buyer has seen the house, but hasn't yet made the decision to buy it. And it is now that being a "Counselor-Seller" really pays off because it's at this point that your buyer will come to you for advice. "Chuck, should I buy this house?" is not an uncommon question. Just remember that the buyer is not just buying our houses, but our reputations as well, so deal with them fairly.

If an investor is new to the real estate business, they may be uncertain about purchasing a house, or confused as to their options. I never push a sale in those cases. I don't want to sell them a house and have them later regret it. I want an ongoing business relationship with that buyer; I'd like them to buy several houses from me. Honest and patient dealings with new buyers will win the day every time.

911 Marketing System for Real Estate Investors ®

The next step is what I call "911 Marketing System for Real Estate Investors®. The goal of the 911 Marketing System is to generate a ton of quality leads that *come to you*, so you can "cherry pick" the best ones. My system shows you how to produce those leads, both with an advertising budget and without. Remember, when I first began, I was broke and had ruined my credit, so an advertising budget wasn't a luxury I had when I started out.

Your success in the real estate investment business largely depends on how good you are at letting your market place know you're in the business. It is essential that you quickly convince buyers and sellers to come to you. If you follow my system, you'll spend minimal dollars with very little effort and make these deals come to you before someone else snatches them up. Your goal is to have leads coming out your ears.

Here's the motto you need to live by: **Always Be On**. Always keep your eyes and ears open because there are deals around you every day that you need to become aware of.

To understand how important marketing is, you first need to understand the role it plays in the real estate investment business. Real Estate is unique in that it doesn't matter how many people you reach, only that you reach the ones that count.

I've discovered that there are essentially five keys to success in real estate investing:

- Locating prospects
- Prescreening prospects
- Constructing and presenting offers
- Follow up
- Selling quickly

The first two are where marketing comes into play.

There are two golden rules you need to remember when advertising in the real estate investment business:

Golden Rule #1: Your seller doesn't care about you, or even the name of your company. I know that's a shock to your ego, but it's really true. The only thing the seller cares about is: *what's in it for them.* They don't want to know if you're married or how the kids are, they don't care where you live or what you drive; they want to know what kind of deal you can put together that will benefit them. That's all. And that's why the largest words in all of my advertising are: WE BUY HOUSES CASH!

Golden Rule #2: Remember **AIDA**

> ➢ Get **ATTENTION** with a strong, benefit-driven headline. You only have a fraction of a second to stop them. If you don't, they're gone forever.
> ➢ **INTEREST** – What's in it for them? It's really all they care about.
> ➢ **DESIRE** – A full list of benefits should be stated and proven. This is where you make your case, and back it up with testimonials and a credibility kit.
> ➢ **ACTION** – What do you want your prospect to do? If you don't tell them, don't expect them to do anything. We can't afford to do "Image Advertising" just to get name recognition, like some big corporations do.

My course covers a *ton* of ways to advertise and market your services, so both buyers and sellers know you're there; but I'll just list a few to give you an idea of some of the things I cover:

- Business cards
- Flyers
- Post cards
- Newspaper ads (not quite the same old thing you see every day)
- Free ads with restaurants and bars or other businesses
- Signs (of all shapes and sizes – I give you terrific examples that work!)
- Contract advertising

I could go on and on, but you get the general idea. I cover how to market with *no* budget (remember, that's exactly how I started!) and *with* a budget for when you start making money.

Using Private Lenders

The next step in my system is how to use Private Lenders for Real Estate Investing®. As you can see, this is also an area of my system that I've had trademarked. When I first came upon the concept of using private lenders to fund my deals, I felt like I'd been smacked between the eyes with a two-by-four. Bear with me and I'll explain.

What is a private lender? Simply put, it's an individual that puts up the money to fund the purchase of a piece of property, and all renovations. There are two ways a private lender gets paid: the first is a percentage of the net profit, the second is interest only payments with the principal amount due at some time in the future. For now, let's examine interest only.

Say for example I borrow $40,000 from Dr. Jones. I agree to pay him 15% simple interest for two years at $500.00 per month, and at the end of the two-year period, Dr. Jones receives his initial investment of $40,000, *plus* he gets to keep all the monthly interest payments. Now, why would I want to pay such a high rate of interest?

In short, because there are a lot of investors around that advertise that they'll buy houses for cash, but the majority of them don't have the cash in hand and are hoping that they can put together a strong enough deal that they can quickly turn it for cash, or find a money partner to come through for them.

Having private money lined up before-hand means you can blow your competition away, because you can close the deal in days, not weeks or months. The result? You can purchase properties at a much deeper discount, because motivated sellers are selling for a reason, and will offer to sell at drastically reduced prices if you can close quickly. In addition to that, you will enhance your reputation as an investor who has money, and can close.

Where do you find potential private lenders? There are a variety of sources, here's just a few:

- CPA's
- Attorneys
- Bankers
- Business owners
- Doctors

The truth is, a private lender could be anybody. My course will teach you how to approach potential private lenders, and how to pitch them with the idea of investing in real estate.

When you make an offer on bank-owned properties, you will be required to include a "Proof of Funds" letter with your offer. Your private lender's banker can write one for them, or whoever handles their cash can do it.

The money referenced by the Proof of Funds letter is deposited into an escrow account, and the monies are dispersed by a title company. In addition, all the paperwork is done by a real estate attorney, so everything is on the up and up, and everyone is protected.

Here's an example of just how powerful the concept of private lending is: about three weeks after I started my marketing campaign, I gained the support of a new private lender that placed $540,000 in an account for me. Within three months I had one million. The following is a copy of the Proof of Funds letter from the bank:

PROOF OF FUNDS LETTER

STERLING | PRIVATE CLIENT GROUP | NATCITY INVESTMENTS

PRIVATE INVESTMENT ADVISORS

[redacted]
Vice President

January 17, 2002

One of my other corporations.

To Whom It May Concern:

Please be advised that The 5th Real Estate Investing Corp. have available funds for use up to $540,000.00. Should have any questions, feel free to contact me at [redacted] It would be my pleasure to assist you.

Sincerely yours,

[redacted]
Vice President
Private Client Group

[redacted] Cleveland, Ohio [illegible]
[redacted]

Fig. 8-1
Proof of Funds letter in the amount of $540,000.

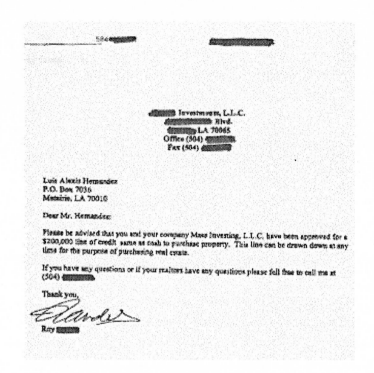

Fig. 8-2
*This is a letter from one of my students that landed a $200,000
Private Lender after learning my system.*

Contract Assigning

Next up is Contract Assigning. This is another great way to earn about *$1,500 per hour*, with a minimum of effort!

What does assigning a contract mean? Simply put, it means that after you've negotiated with a seller, and the contract has been signed, you sell the contract (your position) to a third party (another investor.)

If I had to pick one area of Real Estate Investing that I love the most, it would have to be Contract Assigning. Why? Because it's one of the most lucrative aspects of the business, with very little time commitment.

Contract Assigning is often the wisest, safest and most risk-free way to make money in real estate, because it allows you to bypass the purchasing, renovating and reselling process. Rarely will you have to put up capital or take possession of the property. You can make money without:

> ➤ The liability of owning (unless you take title)
> ➤ Rehabbing the property
> ➤ Marketing the property
> ➤ Qualifying a buyer
> ➤ Selecting tenants, etc.

I routinely sell contracts where I have invested as little as two hours inspecting the property and finding a buyer. The fee I usually charge is $2,000-3,000. Not bad for a couple of hours work!

Now, there *are* downsides to assigning contracts; you can get into trouble if you're sued by the original owner if the person who bought the contract doesn't follow through, or by the buyer, if the original seller refuses to sell or can't deliver a clear title for the property. But I show you in my course how to avoid those pitfalls, and what to do about them if they *do* crop up.

Here are some copies of checks I received from doing Contract Assigning deals:

Figure 8-3
This was a contract assignment. Total time invested: 2 hours.

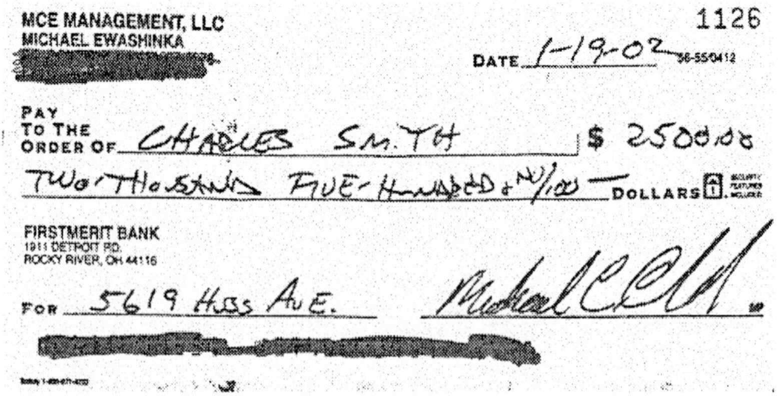

Figure 8-4
Here's another contract assignment. Total time invested: 2 hours (which included an hour for lunch!)

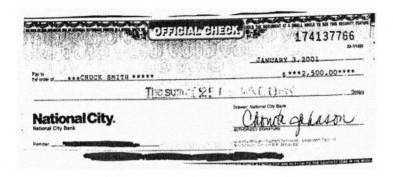

Figure 8-5
This is another contract assignment. Total time invested: 1-1/2 hours.

And keep in mind, these are just a few examples. I do contract assigning frequently, so I get checks like these all the time!

Buying Properties "Subject To"

Like pretty houses? (Who doesn't?) If it's your desire to work with nice houses, in nice neighborhoods, then "Buying Subject To" is right up your alley.

Buying Subject To means *subject to existing financing.* It eliminates closing costs, personal liability when structured correctly, and can eliminate banks from your life for good! Buying Subject To means that you purchase the property without paying off the existing financing. You simply take over the seller's remaining payments and the balance of the old loan.

But what about the "Due on Sale" clause that is in most mortgages, you ask? My course shows you how to avoid that by using a "Land Trust", which results in the lender being unable to call the loan due, unless they want to violate Federal law.

Buying Subject To is only used by the elite of Real Estate Investors. I've seen these same investors pay upwards of $6,000 to attend seminars to learn this technique. It's included in my course as part of another way to develop multiple revenue streams.

What kind of people will sell property Subject To? You'd be amazed!

> ➢ People going through a divorce
> ➢ Job Transfers
> ➢ Can't afford payments
> ➢ Loss of job
> ➢ Death of spouse
> ➢ Poor health
> ➢ Bought another house/making double payments
> ➢ Retiring to another city/state

These are just a few examples; this list is pretty extensive.

You can become wealthy and have a healthy cash flow by Buying Subject To, for a couple of reasons:

1. Only the elite of investors know how to help the people who need to sell Subject To.
2. You can then resell these houses to owner-occupants with no qualifying financing – because *you* are the bank!

The advantages to dealing in pretty houses and Buying Subject To are numerous:

➤ No competition – your competition is looking for fixer-uppers they can steal for next-to-nothing
➤ Little or No Repairs needed – these houses are usually in excellent, move-in condition
➤ You can balance your portfolio
➤ You can start immediately with no money, no partners and no credit – in fact, we professional investors call them "Free Houses" because we get them so easily.
➤ You have an endless supply of sellers
➤ You have an endless supply of buyers (60% of the population cannot qualify for a conventional home mortgage!)
➤ You'll eventually find a home you want to live in

So how can you take title without triggering the Due on Sale clause? In a nutshell, the seller will deed the property to you into what is called a Land Trust. The Garn St. Germain law, the Federal Depository Act of 1982, allows someone to deed a property into a trust for estate planning purposes.

The seller will sign a "Warranty Deed to Trustee", you pick a trustee, have a real estate attorney record the deed, and you control the property. Now, I'm not going to go into too much detail here, because there are legal ramifications and specifics you need to know in order to effectively acquire properties using the Buying Subject To technique – and there's simply not enough room here to teach you all those specifics. If you want to know the finer points of Buying Subject To, take my course.

The great thing about Buying Subject To is that you can frequently get paid by the seller to take the property off their hands! (It happens more often than you might think.)

Let me give you an example of how Buying Subject To can work. (This is from an actual deal.)

The seller contacted me after he learned of an impending job transfer. This was his situation:

! Loan Balance was $138,000
! Monthly payment PITI (Principal, Interest, Taxes, Insurance) was $1,300
! Property appraised for $140,000 and hadn't sold after being listed with a Realtor for 6 months
! Condition of the property was excellent – move in

My offer was:

! Take over loan of $138,000
! Seller make payment for two months after I take possession
! Property was deeded into a land trust
! Seller pays me $2,000 to take the house
NOTE: In the seller's mind, he owed what the property was worth. I simply asked him "How much could you pay me to take your house?" He wrote a check for $2,000.

I immediately ran the following ad in the newspaper:

HOUSE FOR SALE
No Bank Needed/Bad Credit OK/Owner Financing
3 bedroom/1 ½ bath/Move-In condition
$150,000/$1,500 per month/Down Payment Required
Call 440-256-2399

My phone rang off the hook, because no bank was needed, bad credit was OK, it was in a desirable area and it was in move-in condition. I sold the house on a land contract for $150,000 sales price, $7,000 down payment, $1,500 monthly payment for 30 years, with payments to begin within 30 days (move in date.)

My profit on this deal was:

$2,000 upfront from the seller
$1,500 for one payment when I had none yet
$7,000 down payment from buyer

$10,500 Total (immediately), plus $200 a month positive cash flow for the difference between my payment to seller and the payment I collect from the buyer.

The previous deal is one of the simplest and easiest to find when you market your business correctly.
Here's a copy of a check I received from a seller to take three properties off his hands.

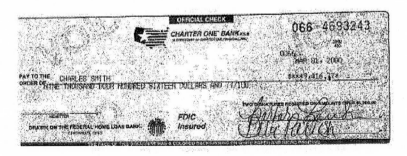

Fig. 8-6
Subject To deal involving three properties

Seller Financing

Now let's talk about another way to both improve your profit margin and accomplish your goal in this business. I'm talking about Seller Financing, which is when the seller assists in one form or another with the financing of the property you're buying from them. For example, the seller acts as a "bank" in a *small* way when they take back a second mortgage on the property, reducing the amount of out-of-pocket money required as a down payment.

Seller financing is at its best when the buyer (that's you) doesn't' require the services of a bank to complete the deal. A seller acts as a "bank" in a *big* way when you (the buyer) don't use a bank at all. When that's the case, there's no better option than seller financing. Here's why:

! No qualifying involved
! There are considerably less closing costs
! You won't be personally liable for the mortgage
! You can often get properties for low (or usually *no*) interest, which results in faster equity build-up
! You can often discount the mortgage

I won't use a bank to buy real estate. I attended a seminar once and the instructor drove home this point exactly. He said, "When you go into a bank, don't step off the tile!" By that, he meant banks are perfectly appropriate places to do *banking*: checking, making deposits, savings accounts, etc. But when you step off the tile, and onto the carpet, like in the loan department, it means you'll be trying to borrow money, and you'll have to qualify for it. And it will cost you.

Let's take a look at some typical bank closing costs. (Cost range on average from 3-10% of the purchase price of the property.)

1.	Credit Report	$	75.00
2.	Appraisal	$	150.00
3.	Survey	$	90.00
4.	Points	$	3,000.00
5.	Origination Fee	$	500.00
6.	Document Preparation	$	100.00
7.	½ of Escrow Fees	$	200.00
8.	Title Policy	$	200.00
9.	Prepaid Interest	$	1,000.00
	TOTAL	$	5,315.00

Five thousand dollars taken right off the top of your deal can *really* eat into your profit margin! Now you see why I won't use banks?

Discounting a Mortgage

Being able to discount a mortgage is one of my primary goals in real estate investing, and you can often do it with a private seller—never with a lending institution. This is how it works:

Let's say you had a first mortgage with the seller for $80,000, and a second mortgage for $20,000. Now, in a properly structured deal, your second mortgage has no payments or small payments with a balloon (payoff date) in seven years or so. After about a year into the deal, you call up the seller and say, "Mr. Seller, I have this second mortgage with you for $20,000 that isn't due for seven years. I came into some money, and wanted to know if I gave you $5,000 today, would you forgive the note?"

Now, maybe you'd have to go up in price, but then again, maybe not. It is staggering just how many people will take the money and run. If the seller counters, and says "Well, I need $10,000 or $15,000 to make it worthwhile," I simply say, "$5,000 is all I have." I may call back later on and try to get them to accept 5 or 6 or $10,000, but you get the point.

I estimate 5% of sellers will do seller financing today. Another 5% will do it in the future. What kind of people consider seller financing?

! The older population – most people over age 60 own their property free and clear, which gives them more options
! Divorcees
! People making two house payments – sometimes they've relocated or just bought another house
! Estate sales – sometimes you can deal here, but usually the heirs want fast cash because it's "found" money. NOTE: this is why you must work <u>all</u> areas of the Real Estate Investment business. This is a potential cash deal.
! Burnt-out landlords – I've bought many properties from landlords who either inherited the house, or didn't know how to manage it.

The reasons people consider holding paper (doing seller financing) are as varied as the types of people who do it. Here's a few of the most common:

! Seller needs a quick sale (maybe they've relocated or they're getting a divorce or they're almost in foreclosure)
! Seller is too old to manage the property
! Seller has no equity
! Seller fears a changing neighborhood. This is one of my favorites for a couple of reasons:
    # If it's only in the seller's mind, I can do seller financing and then later discount the mortgage for cash
    # I can buy for a low cash offer, since the seller is cutting their losses
! Seller's property is in such a state of disrepair (usually in the seller's mind) that he or she feels hopeless. Many times in this case, the seller has been cited for housing code violations and is facing stiff fines and possibly jail. Often the properties are free and clear but the seller can't refinance because of the condition of the house. You're looking at a gold mine in this situation.

Of course, there are situations you need to be careful of, and legal ways to protect yourself, but again, time and space constraints won't let me go into the details here. I cover all those situations and concerns in my course.

Just keep in mind that seller financing is a valuable tool in your arsenal, and can make a huge difference in your bottom line.

Retailing

The last thing I want to cover in this section is retailing. Retailing is the most profitable of all areas of the Real Estate Investment Business, and there's a reason for it: it's because it's the hardest part. Retailing, as far as I've seen in my years in the business, is responsible for putting more people *out* of business than any other area of real estate investing. Finding a bargain property that needs repair is not hard. Finding a bargain property and quick turning it to a cash investor is not all that difficult either. But finding, repairing, locating a qualified buyer, and closing so you can get paid can take time.

I strongly suggest you gain some experience before embarking on this form of investment. After you have some experience in the field, using my system, you'll be ready to tackle retailing. However, I want to caution you to always have a backup plan if you can't retail a piece of property within a certain time frame. There are problems that can occur beyond your control, in the house retailing business.

For example, I know of one investor who has been making payments on *three* empty properties for *six months* because they haven't sold! He refuses to sell them for other than cash, and won't rent them out because he did all the work himself *(big mistake)* and is emotionally attached to them. He forgot the first cardinal rule of this business—that it's a *business!* Emotion can't play a part. Your main goal must be to make money, not lose it.

That's one reason I like to work *all* the facets of the Real Estate Investment Business. If I can't sell a house right away for cash, I simply sell it on a short term (1-3 years) land contract, or rent it out and sell it at a later time. If one of my houses doesn't sell, I just move on to Plan B and make my big money later on.

Please understand that I'm not trying to scare you out of the retailing business. A lot of people have become very wealthy in this business and you can too. I just want to you to be aware of the pitfalls and not have to learn this business in the School of Hard Knocks like I did.

There are several major reasons why people fail in the retailing business:

1. **Buying in the wrong area** – I can't stress this enough: the house <u>must</u> be in an area where people who can qualify for a loan want to live. If the house is a great deal, but in an area that you don't want to retail, just wholesale it and get rid of it.

2. **Buying a house with a bad or outdated layout** – you can't stretch a kitchen to make it bigger. If you think you can put on additions and make money, you need to rethink your position. If that's what you have to do to make the deal palatable, forget it and move on to the next one. The layout of the house should have a flowing effect as you walk through it. If you have to go through one bedroom to get to another, move on to the next deal. You want to rehab a house, not rebuild it.

3. **Paying too much for the house** – This is really self-explanatory. There's an old saying in real estate – You make your money when you buy real estate, not when you sell it. That's so true. Don't get caught in a bidding war. If the property you're looking at isn't a deal, move on. There are a lot of rank amateurs out there overpaying for properties; so you'll see this a lot.

4. **Waiting until the day of closing to line up your rehab crew** – Your goal is to have your workers ready to go the minute you say the house is yours. If you wait until closing, or don't have a written/signed contract to start on time with the necessary work, you'll lose your shirt. As a personal note – if workers can't start on time or finish on time I won't use them again.

5. **Waiting until the house is finished to put it up for sale** – As soon as I have the property in a land trust and it's been cleaned up somewhat on the outside, I put up a "For Sale By Owner" sign. Numerous times I have sold the property *before* I had any serious money into it. That's the idea – make money!

6. **Not getting involved in the selling process** – Whether you plan to use a Realtor, salesperson or not, you MUST KNOW WHAT IS GOING ON WITH THE SALE OF YOUR PROPERTY ON A <u>DAILY</u> BASIS. You simply can't expect someone to be as concerned about you and your profits as you are. I have no problems paying a Realtor his or her full commission, but they *will* earn it. If they don't show the house to pre-qualified people who can purchase my house, they're gone! It is also **your** responsibility to make sure your property is marketed properly.

7. **Not getting involved in the buyer's loan process** – It never ceases to amaze me how many retailing pros out there simply sign a contract with a pre-qualified buyer and wait for it to close, only to find out too late something went wrong. I won't mislead you – I steer my buyers to mortgage brokers I know and trust, not only to get the loan closed, but to keep me continuously informed of the progress. I know what paperwork the mortgage broker needs beforehand, and I see to it that they get it. If my

broker doesn't get up-to-date pay stubs to the loan officer when he says he will, I will pick them up myself and deliver them. If the loan officer isn't requesting items in a timely manner, I'll know about it. People, we are talking about profit checks in excess of $20,000—I have an investment and am not about to allow any person to stand in the way of me making honest money. I'm always professional, however. When people aren't dependable, I'm going to speak up. If they have a problem with this, I WILL NOT DO BUSINESS WITH THEM AGAIN.

8. **Dealing with unreliable, dishonest or incompetent contractors, workers or any other professionals** – this will kill your business faster than anything. If my contractor is not on time and doesn't have a good reason, he's done. If the contractor tries to rip me off, he's done. The same goes for anyone who is hired to do a job. If you are a headache, I won't deal with you.

So where do you find the best retail deals? The basics are the same when retailing as they are for quick turning insofar as locating and purchasing goes.

! I get about 60% of all my retail purchases from the MLS (Multiple Listing Service) accounts. This also means I am depending on my Realtor for the listings. Get a fax machine, and hook it up to a dedicated line. Then establish a good working relationship with a Realtor, who will:

Continuously check the MLS for listings, and fax one in my range and target area to me immediately

Immediately call to check that I received the fax and offer any more hot tips on the property

\#   Immediately submit any offers I want to make

\#   And, of course, have listing agents or brokers contact you *before* the properties are uploaded into the MLS. (In my course, the section on Marketing includes letters and approaches for Realtors.)

!   If you or your Realtor drags your feet on any of these steps, you'll be too late and the house will be gone. I've seen houses sold in just hours.

!   You must be very familiar with your target area(s), and this will come with time. Both you and your Realtor should know what to look for in a listing description. By that I mean there are "Cash Words" in listings that you need to be aware of. (I call them Cash Words because they mean Cash to me.)

\#   Vacant

\#   Addendum required

\#   Subject to short sale

\#   Subject to probate sale

\#   Estate sale

\#   Needs rehab

\#   Needs TLC

\#   Handy-person's special

There are others, but you get the idea.

!   Look for 1-3 family houses. Many seminar instructors preach sticking to single family houses, but there are many beginning investors who want a few quality properties to buy. Don't limit your options. If there is a demand, become the supply.

!   In your follow-up system, you should also have a simple list of properties that have other "cash words" included in the listing that YOU NEED TO CLOSELY WATCH. These include:

\#   Offer withdrawn

\#   Temporarily off the market

\#   Pending

\#   Expired

\#   Back on market

\#   Price reduced
    All of these can mean a deal for you, and cash in your pocket.

I've tried to cover just some of the elements and highlights of my system. In this venue, it's impossible to cover all the aspects and specifics to be found in my course. If you're interested in becoming a successful real estate investor and making more money than you've ever made in your life, you should consider attending either my two-day boot camp – "Chuck Smith's Quick Cash Ultimate Real Estate Boot Camp®" or buy my home study course – "Quick Cash Ultimate Real Estate Investment System ®". Check us out at http://www.chucksmithrealestateseminars.com for more information.

"Though no one can go back and make a brand new start, anyone can start from now and make a brand new ending."
Carl Bard

Chapter 9
Some of My Students' Success Stories (with copies of checks)

Here's where I really have fun! This is where I get to share with you some of my students' success stories. The reasons I like this part are two-fold: 1) it shows you I'm not just tooting my own horn—my system works and my students have the checks to prove it, and 2) there's nothing I like better than helping someone else become successful in this field. If I can do it, *anyone* can do it!

I've chosen a sampling of stories, testimonials and copies of checks my students have sent me: it's by no means all-inclusive—hardly a week goes by that I don't get some sort of communication or "thank you" from a student who's succeeding beyond their wildest dreams. These are some of my favorites.

Chuck,

Since I bought your course 7 months ago, I have had 14 houses deeded to me. I also got 2 more with owner financing. When I returned home from your boot camp I got 3 more houses deeded to me.

Thank You Chuck!

Vito Kostrzewski
Raleigh, NC

Mr. Smith,

I received your course in July 2002. As a result I will be closing on a property in Maui that will net me $50,000 even after our 7% transfer tax. I also wholesaled another property that will net me $3,000.

Thanks,

Jon Tataron, CPA
Maui, Hawaii

Dear Chuck,

As you may recall, we meet at a Ron LeGrand boot camp in 1998 where you did a presentation about your success in Real Estate. I was making okay money in Real Estate at the time but nothing like you were making

I owned several business and all the headaches and risk that goes along with them. I had over 100 employees and 36,000 sq. Ft. of warehouse space along with 5,000 sq. ft. of office space. The only people that had a guarantee that they would get paid were my employees. Don't misunderstand me I enjoyed my businesses and received 2 high profile awards for our accomplishments. We were presented with the National Contractor of the Year award from RSI magazine were I grossed 5 million in sales and Entrepreneur of the Year from Stark County Chamber of Commerce. However, out of all the money my business made per year I took home a very small portion. I was working 16 hour days and all the risks and liabilities. I wanted a business that would not only give me financial independence but time off to enjoy life as well.

I attended countless boot camps and studied many courses on Real Estate but always felt there was something missing. When I heard your presentation I was totally amazed at your system, it ran like a machine much like a franchise does.

I purchased your system and never looked back. Using your system I now average $200,000 per year and believe me I could make more, But I enjoy spending time with my son and enjoying all the other things I was unable to do in my past business life.

I enclosed a few copies of checks as proof.

Thank you very much

Dan Buxton

Fig. 9-1
A letter from one of my students who now makes an average of $200,000 per year. See figures on the following pages of checks from this student (profits checks totaling $75,659.50.)

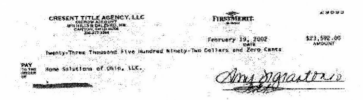

Fig. 9-2
*This was a retail deal – purchased from an estate; had some minor
cosmetic repairs made and sold 2 weeks later to another investor.*

Fig. 9-3
*Same student – this was a retail deal. House was purchased from a
private seller, renovated and sold 4 weeks later to an owner-occupant.*

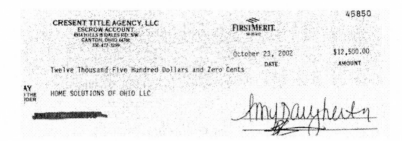

Fig. 9-4
Same student – this was a wholesale deal. Purchased from a bank, and sold 4 days later to another investor.

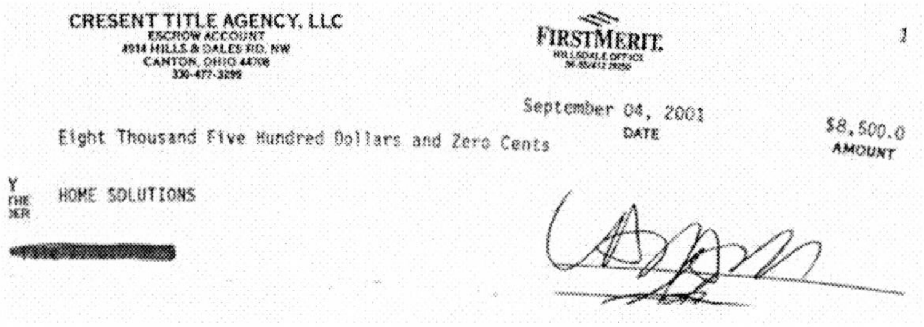

Fig. 9-5
Same student – this was a wholesale deal. Purchased from a bank and sold 6 days later to another investor.

Chuck,

I have had your Quick Cash Home Study Course for 2 months and I wanted to thank you. Your down to earth methods and style have added credibility to an industry full of "want to be investors".

My first deal was a pre-foreclosure that I bought for $90,000 and sold for $140,000 after $10,000 in work. My second was a house I bought for $130,000 and sold 20 days later for $148,900. My best so far is a house I bought for $131,000 and will be closing for a sales price of $199,000.

Thank you so much for all of your support and encouragement. I hope people are smart enough to take advantage of your training.

Darryl Tramonte
Houston, Texas

Chuck,

I received your "Quick Cash Ultimate Real Estate Course" and 10 days later I made $12,500.

Thanks!

Linda Dana
Charlotte, NC

Chuck,
I wanted to write and tell you about two deals I just closed on. One was a house with an ARV of $110,000.
I purchased it on a lease option and got the buyer qualified a few months later. I made $16,232.97 on that
deal. I closed on another property that had an ARV of $350,000. I sold that house and made $54,460.68.
I am a licensed mortgage broker and make a nice income but just wanted to do some deals for extra money.
Your "Quick Cash" Real Estate Course is the absolute best there is. Your coaching program was exactly
what I needed and I can't thank you enough. You can count on me being at your next seminar no matter
what.

Thank You,

Mike McKay

PS.
I eclosed copies of my checks as proof.

Fig. 9-6
Letter from another student.

Fig. 9-7
Purchased on a lease option, and sold a few months later to an investor.

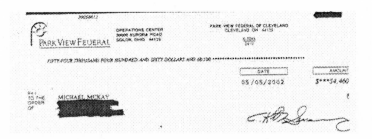

Fig. 9-8
Same student – Retail deal.

Dear Chuck,

Using techniques from your Real Estate course, I recently sold a property for a net profit of $39,000. We are closing soon on another property and will clear $28,000.

Thank you so much for all your help,
Robert Moore

-Former police officer shot 4 times in the line of duty during a gun battle with a robbery suspect. Robert was forced to retire because of his injuries.
Cleveland, Ohio

See more information on Robert's story on the next page.

December 29, 2002

Monterey Investments, Inc.

Dear Chuck Smith:

Chuck, it has been an exciting mentoring program. As a result of your course and personal tele-mentoring I have been able to establish a corporation and learn the techniques to protect my Real Estate Investing Company (Asset Protection). I have also gained insight into the latest real estate strategies and programs and learned ways to acquiring private investors to fund my deals without using my own money and credit. Chuck, this is the best part of your program!

In addition, I am making a deal that will NET me $35,000. I am very excited to have met you and look forward to attending your seminars. I also look forward to growing with you and some day work seminars together. You, have manifested what other proclaim to have done, THE REAL DEALS, THE CHECKS, AND YOU ARE ALWAYS THERE WHEN I NEED YOU. I thank you so much

Sincerely,

Luis Alexis Hernandez
Real Estate Investor

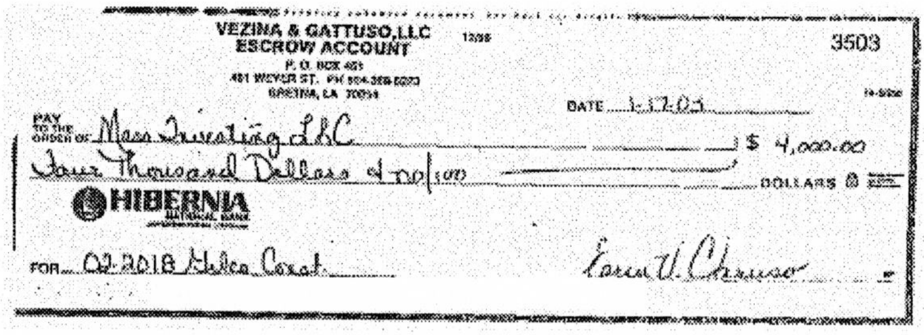

Fig. 9-10
This student made $4,000 in two weeks.

USING THE METHODS TAUGHT IN YOUR COURSE I PURCHASED MY FIRST PROPERTY IN OCTOBER OF 2001 AND HAVE PURCHASED 6 MORE TO DATE. I USED THE METHODS TAUGHT IN YOUR COURSE AND PURCHASED ALL OF THESES PROPERTIES ABSOLUTELY NO MONEY DOWN. LITERALLY NO OUT OF POCKET EXPENSE. ON THE LAST PROPERTY I PURCHASED I WAS EVEN ABLE TO COLLECT A CHECK FOR $10,000.00 AT CLOSING.

I NOW HAVE A NET INCOME OF $2500.00 A MONTH AFTER ALL MORTGAGES AND EXPENSES PAID ON TOP OF MY REGULAR FULL TIME JOB. I HAVE ALSO REACHED ONE OF MY SHORT TERM GOALS OF MAKING MORE IN REAL ESTATE THEN AT MY FULL TIME JOB. I HAVE ENCLOSED A COPY OF THE CHECK FOR $10,000.00 AND A COPY OF MY NET WORTH STATEMENT FROM QUICKEN THAT IS OVER $127,000.00. (MY NET WORTH 6 MONTHS AGO WAS 0)

IN CLOSING I CANNOT EXPRESS HOW MUCH INVESTING IN REAL ESTATE BY USING THE METHODS TAUGHT IN YOUR COURSE HAVE IMPROVED MY PERSONAL AND FINANCIAL WELL BEING?

Sincerely,

THOMAS J FINNERTY

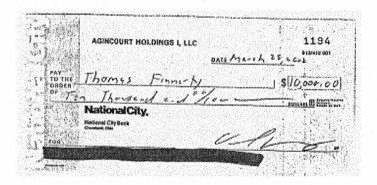

Fig. 9-11
This student increased his net worth from $0 to $127,000 in just six months

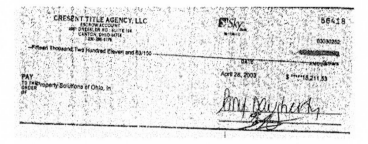

This is a little description of my latest deal. This house was boarded by the city, so it took a little time to track down the owner. The owner of this house deeded us the house for the amount owed which was 6700 dollars. The owner did not want anything to do with this property, he just wanted out! We later sold it for 26,000 dollars which net us over 17,500, and we never ever touched the property!! This check doesn't reflect our 1500 dollar deposit we got from our buyer, and our realtor commission check. Yes, I had listed this property with diana, she is a realtor, "You live and learn," although I did pick up a few new buyers. I also have another property closing next week that is a bank owned property, which will net us 6500 dollars minus a little closing costs. When we get this check Diana and I would like to take you and your wife out to dinner as "THANKS" for putting together a real estate system such as this that ties the whole real estate bussiness together with no hype!!! I hope you will except.

Thanks,

Steve Guttu & Diana Gondeau

Fig. 9-12
This student had my system for 30 days, and made $15,211.53.

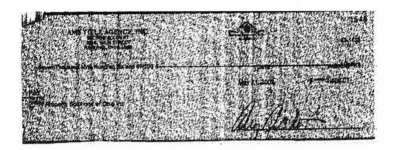

From: Steve Guttu

Here is the other deal that I finally closed on last week. This deal was listed on the MLS. I made an offer, got it accepted, and had it sold the same DAY!!! Diana and I also will get a thousand dollar commission check from Smythe Cramer, because she is a realtor. This is by far the easiest deal we have ever done, because we did not have to find the owner and clear up a title problem like we normally have to do. We have more offers out there that I know we will get accepted!

I will be calling you to try and set up time were we can all get together for dinner, on us!!!

THANKS

Fig. 9-13
Same student. He made $7.906.00 on his second deal.

Chuck,

Holy crap! I have received my fare share of real estate materials over the years, but I have never seen and heard a program so complete and so easy to understand. I received your course yesterday and have made it through Chapter 4. You definitely should congratulate yourself for doing something that I have never seen in business and all of us are looking for, <u>an honest and real program that works today and is not outdated!</u> You also come across on your tapes as a helpful non-pompous guru, very rare! You know Chuck, the only problem I see with this course is it is so good that it seems too good to be true because of so much crap out there. Most of the stuff out there is just too outdated or you go away feeling that the author has conveniently left something important out?

Thank you from the bottom of my heart and I look forward to someday having the honor, if possible, to take you to lunch? Your choice of location, of course. I'll buy!

Best Regards,

Art Deininger

Chuck,

Your Bootcamp was very comprehensive and detailed. I found it very factual to the point that I can put it to work when I get home. I am very glad I found you Chuck!

Thanks,
Ruth Rockey
Palm Springs, CA

Now do you see why I'm thrilled every time I get a letter from one of my students telling me they're succeeding beyond anything they ever expected? It's almost as exciting as succeeding myself. Almost!

*"Where there is a rift in the lute, the business of the lawyer
is to widen the rift and gather the loot."*
– Arthur G. Hays

Chapter 10
Asset Protection

What does that all mean? It means I'm not a lawyer. But I retain one that tells me when to put those kinds of notices in my books.

I firmly believe this chapter may well just be one of the most important chapters in any business book that you'll ever read. Why?

Because you are going to be sued!

If you ignore what I'm going to tell you in this chapter, I can virtually guarantee that at some point in the future you'll be lying awake at night worrying about a lawsuit you've been slapped with, or threatened with. *It doesn't have to be that way!*

If you follow my advice, you can sit back and relax even if you *are* sued, because your asset protection plan will be in place. I know, because I've been sued several times, both before and after my plan was in place.

As I've told you, I experienced great personal pain and injury when a judgment was enacted against me. I lost *everything.* Like I said, if an attorney gets a judgment against you, it's against everything *you own in your own name.*

There are so many ways you can be sued in the Real Estate Investors Business. You can be sued by: tenants, the public, Realtors, contractors, sellers, buyers, partners, you name it, they can sue you. And probably will. I'm really not trying to scare you; I'm trying to tell you the truth as I see it— the truth from my own personal experiences. I've been down that road. I've learned from my mistakes. I'd like to see that you don't make those same mistakes I did.

Once you have a full understanding of asset protection, you can put it into place and not only become wealthy, but hang on to that wealth without fear that some bottom-feeding attorney will come along and take it all away from you.

After I went through the wrenching experience of losing everything I'd built up, I started researching and studying the art of asset protection. I put every property I purchased after that debacle into trusts. I formed a limited partnership, as well as several other types of trusts that we'll talk about shortly.

About two years later, one of my tenants was assaulted by an ex-boyfriend that she had invited into the house. She hired a very good attorney who checked all the country records and discovered that I owned *nothing.* I was only the property manager for the corporation that was hired by the trust to manage the property. Were they confused? You bet. Was that the idea? You bet. I didn't own diddly squat, according to all the legal records. Neither did the corporation. Yet I enjoyed all the benefits of ownership. *And continue to do so to this day,* contrary to what they'd like to see!

Now let's talk a little about the legal entities that can help you with asset protection. Although I'll touch briefly on estate planning, it's not my intention to teach that subject here. I only want to show you how to keep what you earn. After that, you can develop and learn how to control it, even from the grave.

Sole Proprietorship

The sole proprietorship is the simplest and most common form of ownership. If you engage in business without choosing another legal form you're a sole proprietor.

You report your income and expenses on a Schedule C of your income tax return. The gain or loss directly affects any other personal gain or loss.

A sole proprietorship *provides no asset protection*. You are completely responsible for the business and the activities of your employees. Any liability will fall directly on you. All your assets are at risk.

A sole proprietorship doesn't provide any advantage, or disadvantage, for estate planning purposes.

Joint Ownership

Whenever two people own an asset together, they have joint ownership. Joint ownership can take three forms:
1. <u>Tenants in common</u> – the two people each own 50% of the asset. When one dies, his half passes to his heirs or as he otherwise directs.
2. <u>Joint Ownership with right of survivorship</u> – Again, they each own 50% of the asset. When one dies, his half passes to the surviving joint tenant. A will

or other testamentary device has absolutely no effect on this type of ownership.

3. <u>Tenants by the entirety</u> – This special form is created solely by statute, and is a type of ownership exclusive to married couples. A husband and wife in certain states own assets as tenants by the entirety. Each own 50% of the whole entity (e.g. the estate), but not 50% of the asset itself. The ownership interest is an expectancy; the expectancy is that the survivor will inherit the whole when the first person dies.

In a joint ownership you are taxed on your share of the income and expenses of the joint ownership and would report the same on the appropriate portion of your personal income tax return. *Joint ownership does not provide any asset protection.* In some cases, joint ownership may actually *increase* the risk of a loss of an asset. A very common example is when a parent opens a bank account in joint names with a child. The income tax effect is that half of the monies transferred is treated as a gift to the child. A creditor of the child can now attach and take at least one half of the account, in some cases the entire account, since the child is half-owner of the account. Many parents have lost thousands of dollars in this manner.

It is a common tactic as simple estate planning for people to own assets as joint owners with the right of survivorship. Many parents use this form of ownership to pass assets onto their children. When you consider the risks associated with sharing the ownership of assets, I don't recommend this type of ownership.

Corporation

A corporation is a legal entity created under the laws of a particular state by filing certain documents with the state. A corporation can be owned by one or more persons. In some states, one person may be all of the officers in the corporation; in other states, you need at least two people.

The taxation of corporations depends on which portion of the Internal Revenue Code you choose to set up your corporation: subchapter "C" or subchapter "S".

"C" Corporations are treated as a separate tax entity and pay income taxes on any net income. Net income is then distributed as dividends to shareholders, resulting in double taxation. (Once for the corporation, once for the shareholder.) For your purposes, however, you won't allow the corporation to have much net income. You'll spend the money as your salary or pay your other expenses. A "C" Corporation will allow you to deduct more expenses than an "S" Corporation, plus you can create pension and profit-sharing plans with a "C" Corporation that aren't available with an "S" Corporation.

The "S" Corporation isn't treated as a separate tax entity, but does file a separate informational tax return. Your share of the net income or loss is reported on your personal tax return. Because of this "pass through" of losses, the "S" Corporation is particularly well-suited to the ownership of assets or businesses that are producing losses that you would like to use to reduce the taxation of other income.

The tax treatment choice has no effect on the rest of the corporate attributes. The corporation provides tremendous liability protection for the owners of the corporation. Any activity of the corporation in which you are not personally involved will not result in your personal liability. We must be careful how we state this, because I have heard the courts, in recent years, are trying to find additional ways to allow plaintiffs to recover losses or judgments. Shareholders are supposed to be protected from personal liability; however, and this is an important distinction, if shareholders are involved in the operation of the business, they risk getting sued based upon their actions, inactions or management decisions.

All this double-talk, lawyer-speak means that a corporation, or several corporations, are absolutely necessary for your asset protection plan. I want you to be particularly aware that your action as a shareholder and corporate officer can result in your being sued. Now, just because you're being sued doesn't mean you'll lose, or that the plaintiff should win, but you need to be prepared in case they do.

For estate planning purposes, the stock in the corporation will usually be owned by a person's living trust. If you start gifting some of the corporation's stock to your children, you can help reduce any estate tax problems you may have. If you have a separate corporation owned by your children that provides services or equipment to your corporations, you can pay tax-deductible amounts to the children's corporation. These amounts are not part of your estate, and are safe from the claims of creditors.

A single corporation does not improve your estate planning. Multiple corporations with a variety of ownership will improve your estate planning. Creating and using corporations is relatively simple, and is usually an integral part of an estate plan.

Partnerships

When two or more people enter into a business activity, they have, intentionally or otherwise, formed a partnership. Partnerships can be something as simple as a verbal agreement. These types of partnerships can be the most dangerous, because they often end in disputes about money and responsibility for work to be done. If you're considering entering into a partnership, you <u>must</u> have a written agreement. The agreement needs to be very specific: cover everything you can think of from how the money is to be divided to how the partnership will be dissolved when one partner wants out. If you don't hammer out all the details in advance, and get them in writing, they'll come back around later to bite you in a painful place.

A partnership files a separate informational tax return, but doesn't pay taxes. You report your share of the gain or loss on your personal income tax return.

The partnership provides you with very little asset protection. Partners are usually not personally liable for the debts of the partnership, but they *can* be sued personally and can be held liable to the full extent of their personal assets.

A partnership doesn't provide much assistance for use in estate planning.

Limited Partnership

The limited partnership is formed by written agreement between one or more general partners and one or more limited partners. A certificate of limited partnership is then filed with the state in which the limited partnership is formed.

The general partner is in control of the management of the limited partnership. The limited partner does not have any participation in the management of the partnership.

The limited partnership files a separate tax return, but doesn't pay any taxes. You report your share of the gain or loss on your personal income tax return.

The limited partnership *provides tremendous asset protection*. If the limited partnership is sued, the general partner is personally liable beyond the partnership assets. The limited partner is *not* liable beyond the partnership assets. Basically, the limited partners are as safe as the shareholders in a corporation.

The additional protection is provided in the following manner: a limited partnership interest cannot be attached, taken or otherwise controlled or disposed of by a creditor. The creditor's only possible way to attack your limited partnership interest is to obtain a court ordered "changing order." The changing order is a lien against the limited partnership interest which allows the creditor to be paid from any distribution to the limited partner. The creditor must be paid in full before the limited partner receives any money.

The charging order does not give the creditor the right to the net income of the partnership. In a properly crafted limited partnership, the general partner has the sole discretion regarding the distribution or retention of partnership income. Accordingly, when a charging order exists, you probably wouldn't want to distribute the income, particularly since the general partner can receive fees and expenses from the management of the partnership affairs.

Now, pay attention, because this next part is the part I love! The Internal Revenue Code requires that partners pay income tax on the net income of a partnership, even if the partners don't actually receive any money. For example, if you own one-half of a partnership that shows a net income of $200,000, you would pay taxes on $100,000, *even if you receive none of that money, or only a part of it.*

The courts have ruled that the creditor with a charging order is required to pay taxes on the share of the net income that the limited partner would have received if the general partner allowed the distribution. If a creditor has a charging order against your limited partnership interest, then the *creditor* would be required to pay taxes on the $100,000, even though the creditor has not received any money.

This allows you to completely turn the tables on a judgment holder. These people will look like the proverbial deer caught in the headlights. Can you imagine the conversation when the plaintiff's lawyer explains to the plaintiff that not only is the plaintiff not going to receive any money, but now the plaintiff must pay taxes on the $100,000? You now have the opportunity to be in control of the situation, rather than being controlled by the plaintiff.

The limited partnership also provides us with tremendous opportunities for reducing the federal estate tax burden. If I asked you how much $1,000,000 in cash was worth, you'd immediately respond with the answer: $1,000,000. Now if I asked you to place a value on a limited partnership interest that owned $1,000,000 in cash, your answer would change. As a limited partner, you don't control the management of the assets of the partnership, and your interest is not easily transferable. This substantially reduces the value of the limited partnership interest from the value of the assets owned by that interest. As a result, your limited partnership interest may be worth only 60-70% of the actual value of the asset.

The Internal Revenue Service has been forced to accept this reduced valuation for federal estate tax returns. You now have the ability to reduce the taxable value of an estate from $2,000,000 to $1,200,000 simply by creating limited partnerships. You can potentially save hundreds of thousands of dollars.

You also have the ability to transfer part of the limited partnership interest to your children. This will reduce your assets for your estate. By transferring the limited partnership interest, however, you don't give the children any rights of control over the assets. By controlling the general partner, you retain control of the assets until you choose to relinquish them, or you die.

Your asset protection plan should definitely include one or more limited partnerships.

Limited Liability Company (LLC)

The limited liability company is a hybrid between the corporation and the limited partnership. This legislative creation is currently available in all fifty states and the District of Columbia. The purpose of the limited liability company is to provide the same limited liability for business owners as a corporation, without all the corporate requirements.

The tax status depends upon the exact method of formation of the limited liability company. The current Internal Revenue Service ruling allows the limited liability company to be treated as a partnership. In certain circumstances, the limited liability company could also be treated as a corporation under subchapter "C". The only law regarding the tax treatment comes from the most recent revenue rulings issued by the Internal Revenue Service. The IRS is still reviewing the tax treatment, and may change its previous decisions.

This is the first of two areas to watch with limited liability companies: any change in tax treatment could severely impact your personal tax situation.

The second area of concern is that since they are relatively new, protection under LLC's has not yet been fully tested in lawsuits in each state and at the federal level. The goal is to have the LLC provide you with the same asset protection as the limited partnership. But while the limited partnership is time-proven, and more importantly, court-tested, the limited liability company doesn't yet have the track record that I can point to and assure you that everything will be ok.

These concerns don't mean I'm telling you not to use limited liability companies. They *do* mean I'm not yet comfortable endorsing LLC's. I would feel better if 1) the IRS tax code dealt specifically with the tax treatment of the limited liability company, and 2) several court battles had been fought and appealed to higher state or federal courts. That's coming, as a few cases work their way through the system, but until I see some real concrete evidence, like current court rulings, I'll hold back on complete endorsement of LLC's

If you do choose to use the limited liability company, you <u>must</u> keep current on all the changes in your state laws and the tax treatment.

Living Trust

A living trust is a specific type of *inter vivos* trust which is formed to be used while you are still alive. The living trust is revocable or terminable during your lifetime.

The trust is created with you and your spouse as trustees and beneficiaries during your lifetimes. The trust does not file a separate tax return, and your personal tax return doesn't change.

The main reason to form and use a living trust is to avoid the perils and problems of probate. Because you choose a successor trustee when you form the trust, the successor trustee is *immediately* in charge of the trust upon your death. The successor trustee doesn't require much assistance from an attorney, and doesn't require court approval to manage the trust affairs.

This immediate action by the successor trustee assures:

1. Your family is taken care of and money is made available to them quickly.
2. Your business interests are not set adrift until the court approves an executor and the attorney decides to act
3. The full value of your assets is maintained, instead of being greatly diminished by your death and the ensuing confusion, and
4. The costs of administering the estate are greatly reduced.

The only asset protection provided by the living trust is through the splitting of the ownership of assets between the husband and the wife. The court will not allow the creditor of one spouse to attack the assets of the other spouse.

The living trust allows us to achieve a very high level of estate planning. A property crafted and funded trust is set up to pass the maximum possible assets through the trust with the least possible taxes being paid. <u>Everyone must use a living trust as part of his asset protection plan.</u>

Married couples cannot afford to be without a living trust. When correctly used, the living trust will also double the available federal estate tax deduction usually claimed by most married couples.

Land Trust

The land trust is a type of *inter vivos* trust which is used primarily to hold the title to real estate. The primary purposes of the land trust are to hide your ownership of real estate, and to provide the initial layer of asset protection.

The land trust is formed by the trustee and the beneficiary executing a trust agreement and a deed being recorded to transfer the real estate into the trust. The trust then becomes the legal owner of the real estate and the beneficiary becomes the owner of the trust. (Got that?)

The land trust does not file a separate tax return, and your personal income tax return does not change. The transfer of currently-owned real estate into a land trust does not have any tax implications.

You will only place one parcel of real estate into each land trust. This provides the maximum asset protection because it causes each parcel of real estate to be titled separately.

We want this scenario because when you lose a lawsuit, the resulting judgment is automatically a lien against any and all real estate titled in your name. If a judgment is entered against you, and no real estate is titled in your name, then the judgment does not become a lien against any real estate.

If the lawsuit involved one of the specific pieces of real estate, the judgment against the land trust would only result in a lien against the single piece of property titled to that land trust. Your other real estate holdings would not be liened. A judgment holder now has to work much, much harder to collect anything from you.

If you're an active real estate investor, this gives you the ability to sell or refinance other pieces of real estate without being bothered by the judgment against you or the lien against the single property. Without using a land trust, a single judgment would lien *all* of your real estate and prevent you from doing business.

The privacy issue is important because
> 1. You never want anyone to know the full extent of your business dealings, and
> 2. If the potential plaintiff and his attorney aren't certain you have any assets to go after, they may not even file suit.

It is *essential* that you use land trusts to own each separate piece of real estate.

Irrevocable Life Insurance Trust

The irrevocable life insurance trust is a type of *inter vivos* trust created to own your life insurance policy during your lifetime, to collect the proceeds of the insurance upon your death and to either hold in trust or distribute the money to your heirs.

The main reason for creating the trust is to prevent the proceeds of your life insurance from being taxed for federal estate tax purposes. Life insurance proceeds are not taxed for income tax proceeds. The proceeds are included, however, in the value of your estate if you own a policy when you die.

If the dollar value of the policy increases the total value of your estate so that it exceeds the amount you can pass through without paying federal estate taxes (currently $1,000,000) then you need to remove the life insurance from your ownership.

The irrevocable life insurance trust will accomplish this. In some cases, transferring the policy ownership to your spouse may accomplish the same thing.

Because this trust is irrevocable and would contain appropriate spendthrift provisions, the trust assets are very safe from your creditors and the creditors of the beneficiaries.

Umbrella Policy

Another critical component to asset protection is to buy <u>at least</u> a million dollar umbrella policy. Most people think umbrella policies are just for the rich, are too complicated to coordinate with your existing liability coverage, and cost too much. All not true.

First off, in this day and age, with juries routinely giving awards and judgments in the millions of dollars, and as we've seen, *anyone* can be sued for almost anything. You don't have to be rich to get sued, or to get a huge financial judgment against you.

Anytime you go into business, you'll need to take out business liability insurance. Most business liability policies come with a liability limit of around $300,000—some are higher, but that's the standard amount issued. An umbrella policy takes over when the underlying limit (in this case $300,000) is exceeded. For example, if you get a judgment against you for $750,000, your basic liability policy would pay the first $300,000, then the umbrella policy would pick up the additional $450,000.

The cost isn't prohibitive; maybe a few hundred dollars a year, and your current liability insurance agent probably offers umbrella coverage as well. If not, there are plenty who do.

Keep in mind that insurance companies often retain the best and brightest attorneys on their own staff—the better to defend you and themselves in a suit. Even if you are sued, the insurance companies will sometimes settle out of court, before the case even goes to trial, if they can negotiate a reasonable settlement.

Irrevocable Children's Trust

The irrevocable children's trust is a type of *inter vivos* trust created to transfer assets to your children without them being in control of the assets. This trust is created and initially funded by you.

The trust files a separate tax return. The tax treatment depends upon the age of the children. The income of children over age fourteen is taxed separately based upon their individual tax rates. The income of younger children is taxed at the same rate as their parents.

The trust provides for superior asset protection, although you lose control of the assets and can never get them back. The trust, however, can choose to loan you money should you desire to borrow from it.

The irrevocable children's trust can provide you with great asset protection and a way to spread income to the children. The downside is loss of control and relinquishing the assets forever. The trust is a great tool when properly used in situations where the parents do not need access to assets, or the income they might provide.

These are some of the methods of asset protection I discuss in my full course. Clearly, there is a great deal more detail to each of these plans; plus you need a competent and trustworthy attorney to set up some of the more complex verbiage in some of these entities. Find yourself a good lawyer (no, that's *not* an oxymoron!) and begin protecting yourself and your assets!

If you limit your choices only to what seems possible or reasonable, you disconnect yourself from what you truly want, and all that is left is a compromise.
- Robert Fritz

Chapter 11
Personal Development

Life is about overcoming obstacles. It's about never giving up, because if you give up, you're done for. They might as well bring on the funeral hearse, because it's all over.

I want to talk about personal development. Not like some inspirational, self-help guru who spouts all that psychological mumbo-jumbo, but with some straightforward, common sense advice. I'm going to use several of my favorite quotes and stories in this chapter, as a way to illustrate what I'm talking about, because this is a critical component to you taking the information in this book, or in my course, and putting it into action in your own life.

Here's a revolutionary thought: *You are responsible for your own destiny.* That's an important point, so let me repeat it: *You* are responsible for your own destiny. Think about that for a moment. The entire responsibility for your life rests on your own shoulders. That's an incredibly liberating thought for some, a very scary concept for others.

No matter what's gone on in your life up to this point, no matter how horrendous it's been, no matter what experiences you've been through, no matter what people have done to you for all your years on earth, it's how you *react* to those events that will determine how successful you'll be in life. And I'm not talking just financial success, but your success as a human being.

Ok, maybe you had horrible parents, maybe you were sexually abused or raped at a young age, or grew up so poor you went to bed hungry on a regular basis, or were beaten daily, or tormented by bullies. Whatever. Here's a piece of advice: *Get over it!* Blame only goes so far. You can't walk around with your head in the clouds, acting like a jerk, because of something that happened to you when you were six. Well, that's actually not true, you can do that; people do it all the time. But if you're really interested in fixing what's wrong with your life, you'll stop playing the blame game, and accept the fact that it's up to you, *and you alone*, to take responsibility for your life, put aside whatever happened in the past, and focus on building a future for yourself.

It's not your parent's fault if your life is a mess. It's not your neighbor's fault, or your spouse's; it's *yours!* And until you realize that, and deal with it, things aren't going to change.

> *Forget about blame, just concentrate on the issues. Don't look at others, look at yourself.*
> *-Sun Tzu, Chinese philosopher*

Regardless of where you end up in life, you did it.

If you had a briefcase that contained a million dollars in cash, and I tried to take it from you, how hard would you fight to keep it?

Answer: until you could no longer fight, until your last breath, until death. That's probably a fair and accurate statement for most people, wouldn't you agree?

So why is it that the average person will let the person closest to them, often the most miserable, broke and ignorant person around, talk them into quitting without even the smallest amount of resistance? I see it happen all the time.

There's a phenomenon I call "social flushing". It means that, overtly or otherwise, consciously or subconsciously, your friends, family, associates, those closest to your or in your social set, will tell you, by word or by deed, that you *can't* do something, or *shouldn't* do something. "*It won't work. It can't happen. Don't go there*". There's a whole variety of things they say, a whole set of negative reactions and verbiage they use to let you know that *there's no way you can be a successful person*. Sometimes they don't even realize they're doing it. Sometimes they do. <u>*Sometimes you'll do it to yourself*</u>. STOP. Right now.

You have a perfect right to be successful, both financially and personally. Don't let the dream stealers make you believe otherwise. *Don't let yourself believe it*. It may come as a surprise, but it's almost a given that as you grow financially and personally, those who *aren't* growing will feel uncomfortable. And because *they* feel uncomfortable, they'll try to drag you back down to their level. Develop a hearing problem when you're around such people; tune them out, ignore their defeatist message, do whatever it takes to not listen to what they're saying. As far as I'm concerned, these types of people might as well put a gun to your head and pull the trigger. Whether it was intentional or an accident, the end result is the same: your dreams are dead, and so are you. In my book, dream stealing equals a felony.

Their rationale for sabotaging you in this manner, even subconsciously, is because if *you're* moving forward, growing and developing and trying to improve your life, *they might have to do the same things just to keep up with you*. And it's much easier for people to lay around on their complacent, whining butts and blame others for the state of their lives, than to get up and actually go work hard to make the changes necessary to improve their lot in life. Hard work? What's that? *We don't want to work hard, we just want to complain!*

> *One of the most shocking lessons in life is the discovery that not everyone wishes you well. There is a surprising amount of jealousy, envy and resentment directed at high achievers in every field. The more you try to do and the more you do, the more you will be subjected to it.*
>
> *– Dan Rather*

I want you to get a sign. Make one up on the computer, or have a friend make one for you; hand-letter it if you need to. But I want you to put a sign up, either near your desk, or in your office, or bedroom, or *somewhere* that you'll see it every day. It needs to say simply this:

NO WHINING ALLOWED!

Every time a loved one, or a co-worker, or a family member, or a friend, tries to lead you down the path of *"You can't do that"*, you either point to that sign, or mentally visualize it. Don't let them tell you your dreams are unattainable. *They aren't.* I'm not saying someone is going to hand them to you on a silver platter—you'll have to get up and go work for them, but you *can* succeed!

> *Twenty years from now you will be more disappointed by the things you didn't do than by the ones you did. So throw off the bowlines. Sail away from the safe harbor. Catch the trade winds in your sails. Explore. Dream. Discover.*
> *– Mark Twain*

Intelligence is a valuable attribute to have in this world, but it's not necessary to succeed. Without the will to succeed behind it, intelligence means nothing. The world is full of really smart people who are complete failures in life.

Beauty is a good thing to have, but it doesn't guarantee success either. You can be superficially attractive, but you can't base your success in life on it. Even Hollywood stars get old and wrinkled at some point. And look at how many people go to Hollywood expecting to become a big star, and end up with nothing.

Ambition is a great quality, but it won't do you any good without the drive to succeed behind it. I personally know a lot of ambitious people; they always have plans and goals and schemes and desires, but they run around like the proverbial chickens with their heads cut off, and never accomplish anything. They're so scattered and disorganized they can't focus on what they really want to accomplish.

You must start first with a belief in yourself. I'm not talking about a blind, stubborn, mule-headed obstinacy that won't listen to reason—that's not necessarily the way you want to go either. I'm talking about a calm and confident belief that the path you're proceeding on will be the right one for you; a conviction that no matter the odds and no matter the objections, you will succeed at whatever task it is that you have in front of you. It's not a defiant or rebellious attitude, simply an unshakable will to succeed.

In my opinion, determination is probably the single biggest factor in deciding whether or not you're going to make a success of your life. With determination, you can overcome any hurdles, any setbacks, any roadblocks *anyone* throws up in front of you.

Let me give you a real quick history lesson that shows you what I'm talking about. Abraham Lincoln is one of the most beloved and revered figures in American history, but he had a helluva life. And most people don't know everything he overcame to become President.

- ➢ He failed in business in 1831
- ➢ He was defeated for state legislature in 1832
- ➢ He tried another business in 1833. It failed.
- ➢ His fiancée died in 1835.
- ➢ He had a nervous breakdown in 1836.
- ➢ He ran for Congress in 1843 and was defeated.
- ➢ He tried again in 1848 and was defeated.
- ➢ In 1855 he tried running for the Senate. He lost.
- ➢ The next year he ran for Vice President, and lost.
- ➢ He ran for the Senate again in 1859 and lost.
- ➢ In 1860, he ran for the Presidency, and was elected the 16th President of the United States.

The difference between history's boldest accomplishments, and it's most staggering failures is often, simply, the diligent will to persevere. Determination. To succeed at all costs, and against all odds.

I've attended Real Estate seminars all over the country, and it never ceases to amaze me how few people actually *do* anything with what they've learned. I've personally watched people use a credit card to pay seminar fees in excess of $20,000, only to talk to the same people a year or two later and discover that they've done absolutely *nothing* with the knowledge and skills they learned in that expensive seminar.

It drives me crazy, because these are the same people that whine and moan and complain about not having the things in their lives they really need: more time or money or whatever it is they're lacking. If they'd take all that energy they use to whine, and apply it to accomplishing their goals, there's no limit to what they could do!

Let me tell you a little bit more about my life today. Just a few years ago, I was a street cop trying to support my wife and four kids on a crummy salary. I worked part-time jobs and 16-hour shifts at the police department just to survive. Today, I can take my family out to dinner every night, if that's what I wanted to do. We live in a nice house, drive nice cars, and can afford to live the American dream. We own a luxury condo in South Carolina that overlooks the ocean. I sometimes now make more in a week than I previously made in a year. I'm not telling you all this to impress you, but to convey to you how my life has changed by making personal development a way of life.

I'm living today the way that maybe 2% of the people in our country live. But in order to get there, I had to change my entire mindset to *not accept what the other 98% of the people in this country will settle for.* Compromise in this area is simply unacceptable. I wanted more. And I went out and got it. *And you can, too!*

But in order to do that, you <u>have</u> to make personal development and successful strategies a *way of life.* You are capable of so much more than you can believe. When you get past the fear of failure or looking bad and realize that you only truly fail when you quit, then what you can achieve is nothing short of amazing.

There are any number of positive personal achievement programs out there. I'm not talking about the positive thinking or "Rah, Rah, I'm Happy, You're Happy" crap. I'm talking about some programs that actually give you the tools to help turn your dreams into reality. In the reference section of this book you'll find a list of some of the programs I recommend. I don't get anything for promoting these programs; I'm just passing them along to you because I've used them, and they've helped me.

> *What every man needs, regardless of what his job or the kind of work he is doing, is a vision of what his place is and may be. He needs an objective and a purpose. He needs a feeling and a belief that he has some worthwhile thing to do. What this is no one can tell him. It must be his own creation. Its success will be measured by the nature of his vision, what he has done to equip himself, and how well he has performed along the line of its development.*
>
> *– Joseph M. Dodge*

There's a school of thought that if you took all the money in the world and evenly distributed it, it would be back in the hands of the same people who originally had it within five years. I think there's some truth to that. Once you've learned how to create wealth, even if you lose it, you'll get it back.

Once you've learned how to be successful in life, and have accepted responsibility for your financial and personal accomplishments, you'll always follow that path. I'm not saying that there won't be hurdles and setbacks; that's the nature of life. But learning how to cope, learning how to deal with problems, learning how to *succeed* is a habit or behavior that you can become skilled at, with a little practice.

Don't ever give up on your dreams. You're dead in the water if you do.

All people are self-made. Only successful people admit it. *- Ron Le Grand*

"You are now at a crossroads. This is your opportunity to make the most important decision you will ever make. Forget your past. Who are you now? Who have you decided you really are now? Don't think about who you have been. Who are you now? Who have you decided to become? Make this decision consciously. Make it carefully. Make it powerfully.
Anthony Robbins

Chapter 12
Looking Toward the Future

Well, there you have it. That's pretty much the highlights, and low-lights, of my life to date. What have I learned?

I've learned that life is tough; with tough lessons that need to be learned. *Everyone* goes through tough times. The key is to take away a key lesson from every major experience you go through; good or bad. Don't keep making the same mistakes over and over again. Learn from past mistakes and move on.

I've learned that family and friends matter—that they stand by you when the sky is falling and your world is coming unglued. And they'll be there for you when the good times roll, and you're absolutely sure you're King of the World.

I've learned that personal development and professional growth are crucial to success. *My* success, anyway. They say "Only when a student is ready will the teacher appear." I've had several teachers and mentors point me toward the right path, and give me a much-needed push in that direction, and I thank them for their encouragement and support.

I've learned that no matter what happens in life, *never give up.* That's probably become my strongest mantra. Don't lose hope, don't ever throw in the towel; don't quit. Once you lose hope, you become powerless to change your life. And that's a real tragedy, because with determination and persistence, and accepting personal responsibility, you can turn your life around and begin living your dreams. I've talked a lot in this book about the teachers and mentors I've encountered along the way, and I almost feel like I have an obligation to pass along some of that encouragement and knowledge. It's like throwing a pebble in a pond—the ripple effect in people's lives is nothing short of amazing. If you'll allow me to become a teacher and mentor to you, you can see the same sort of astonishing turn-around in your life that I experienced.

This chapter covers the boot camp and seminar training that I offer, along with some testimonials from my own mentors and teachers. If you're interested in living like the top 2% of the people in this country, this is the place to start. If you want to quit that job you hate and start providing your family with the *real* luxuries of life, begin here. Quit fooling around with a job or career that isn't getting it done, and start living the kind of life you've always dreamed about.

Every once in a while a student really gets it and becomes a first class student. I've watched Chuck Smith go from a police officer to a world class real estate entrepreneur making over $500,000 per year almost overnight. It's a straight to the point masterpiece worth its weight in gold. Consider yourself lucky Chuck is about to enter your life.

Ron LeGrand

Home Study Course

Picture yourself telling your boss: "I no longer need the money you're paying me, and this job is taking up too much of my valuable time. I want to enjoy life!"

How many business opportunities have you looked at? Ten? Fifteen? Twenty? Sure, there might be people making money in all of them... but there's always something that doesn't quite match up, isn't there? Maybe the company was a franchise. Maybe they just wanted to grab your life savings—force you to quit your job and work 80 hours a week not even knowing if the business would succeed. Or maybe you needed good credit to get one of those huge start-up loans that leave you deep in debt for life, even after the business goes down the tubes.

Or worse, maybe it was one of those Multi-Level Marketing schemes that force you to annoy your friends, neighbors, relatives and anyone you've ever met in your life by trying to sign them up, and you're not even making money!

Well, STOP IT.

You're about to learn a business concept that is creating a mini-revolution all across the country and giving thousands of people the ability to create their own wealth, and most importantly, a steady, heavy cash flow from their living room.

Here are some of the benefits of choosing my system:

- **Set your own hours** – Start part-time and earn while you learn. Match or exceed your "real" job's regular income before you walk away from it.
- **No fixed expenses to worry about** – Work out of your home, or off the dining room table, if you want. Enjoy the convenience and tax breaks of having a home-based business without the worry of employees, or a huge overhead.
- **You operate using a proven system** – But with NO franchise fees! You keep all the profits!
- **Enjoy a pleasant, interesting white-collar workday** – You'll be the CEO of your own business. It's briefcase work, not LUNCH BUCKET WORK!
- **Flexibility** – Go it alone, or with a partner. Work full or part-time. Work on weekdays or weekend. Make a few thousand dollars, or a six-figure income. It's all up to YOU!
- **Make instant profits** – Here's one that *I* thought was impossible when I started, but it's true: make thousands of dollars on your very first transaction, and do it instantly.
- **A business you can be proud of** – No Multi-Level system here. You can earn huge amounts of money and people will thank you for doing business with them.
- **No long-term personal debt** – You can start with zero cash, even lousy credit and no job. If you need to throw your own money and credit into this business, you're doing it wrong.
- **No glass ceiling** – This is a big factor in attracting people to this business. Let's face it, in the real world,

discrimination still exists. Using my system, it doesn't matter what your race is, what your gender is or where you came from. The sky's the limit. It's all up to YOU!

➢ **No home repair skills needed** – Using my system, <u>WE DON'T DO REPAIRS!</u> We hire other people to do them. Most of the time, I sell houses "AS IS" and don't even touch them.

➢ **No Land lording allowed** – You won't be a landlord. Enough said!

My system is unique because not only do I dissect what really works and *why*, but I look at what *doesn't work,* and why. This is a close lesson in realism, not pie-in-the-sky theories.

Exactly what is my system and what does it cover? You'll learn several ways to make money in real estate. I know some real estate agents and other investors try to make it all sound confusing, but basically ALL Quick Turn transactions fall into one of only a few categories that I cover in detail in my course.

1. **Wholesaling** – Finding bargains and selling them to bargain-hunters. Trust me, they'll be begging you to sell to them.
2. **Contract Assigning** – This is like wholesaling, but even quicker. You can literally make $1,500 to $3,000 with only one hour of your own time invested.
3. **Retailing** – Basically this is renovating the same bargains you would have wholesaled and selling them for top price. This is very profitable, but my system will have you get into this part of the

business slowly, because it's more difficult and you need a little experience before tackling it. However, depending on how quickly you progress, you could be cashing checks for $25, $30 or even $50,000.

4. **Getting the Deed** – This is simply taking ownership of nice houses in great neighborhood by taking over existing loans. And the loans don't have to be assumable. This doesn't involve giving the seller money and doesn't require credit or qualifying. My system even teaches you how to get the seller to pay you to take their house ... I'm NOT kidding! These houses are always in move-in condition.

5. **Sandwich leases** – In those cases where the seller won't deed you the house, we can still control houses and make huge profits. Not to mention developing monthly income streams, and much more.

To say Chuck Smith and his real estate investment system are very impressive would be an understatement! Chuck Smith's Quick Cash Ultimate Real Estate Investment System will give you the knowledge and the power to build wealth you never thought possible! Chuck Smith gives you that knowledge in one complete package!

Brian Tracy
(One of the world's leading authorities on personal and business success)

Each of the methods in my system have features and benefits that appeal to different types of people, and that's ok! That's why this business is so great: YOU pick what suits you and make money without the stress and strain of an imperfect fit. I've created a complete system around each of these different facets of the business that will give you a perfect fit for your personality and preferences, and that, my friend, is how you are going to enjoy your work!

What's included in my system:

➢ **Building and Cultivating a Buyers List ®**
   Taught nowhere else. So powerful, I trademarked it!
➢ **Contract Assignment**
   I make $1,500-$2,000 per hour doing this.
➢ **Wholesaling**
   I teach you to sell to a certain type of buyer. Most of what other courses teach you is DEAD WRONG! I make an average of $10,000 per deal. Who would you rather listen to?
➢ **Retailing**
   I have you slowly get into this aspect of the business. Why? Because you need some experience so you

don't lose your shirt. Besides, you can make a ton of money without ever retailing one house. When you're ready, it's all covered in detail. I've made as much as $68,000 net profit on one deal. Need I say more?

➢ **911 Marketing for Real Estate Investors** ®
I've spent a small fortune to be personally mentored by Dan Kennedy, the best in the USA. I don't look for deals, they come to me. This portion is divided into two sections: marketing with no budget, and marketing with a budget.

➢ **Tough Cop Contractor Management System** ®
I will make you a tough cop so you won't get overcharged a penny.

➢ **Owner Financing**
I'll teach you how I made $47,000 on ONE DEAL.

➢ **Getting the Deed/Selling the Deed**
I teach you how to get sellers to deed you pretty houses, and then turn around and sell the deed.

➢ **Lease Options**
Covered in detail.

➢ **Schematic Diagrams**
I include schematic drawings that break down the individual components of a house. You can be so dumb you can't spell Home Depot, but using my system you'll function like an expert!

➢ **Private Lenders for Real Estate Investors** ®
Forget about hard money loans, credit lines or equity loans. I teach you in detail how I fund a multi-million dollar real estate business. You get all of my tools: brochures, letters, script for a cassette tape, etc. I raised 1 million dollars in 3 months using the same system I perfected.

➢ **Asset Protection System**
I teach you how to bullet-proof your wealth. Everything, from Land Trusts to Corporations and LLC's are covered in great detail.

There are two free bonuses with my Home Study Course:
1. CD Rom with all the real estate forms you need for this system. Just put the CD in your computer, and fill in the blanks.
2. Radio Interview with Chuck Smith – listen as I'm interviewed on "Business Talk"

There are a lot of broke, amateur investors out there. Using my system, you won't waste your time learning by trial and error, making expensive mistakes, generally looking like a fool. My system leaves other investors in the dust. I guarantee you'll hit the ground running.

To order the Home Study Course today and begin living the life you've always dreamed of, log onto my website: http://www.chucksmithrealestateseminars.com or call 1-866-474-2432.

Quick Cash Ultimate Real Estate Boot Camp

A few times a year I put on a two-day live boot camp, where you can learn the most powerful strategies and techniques ever created that make up the system I use.

This live event is about you and your family's future; about you not working for someone else the rest of your life. Why slave all year for an income that you could make in a few real estate deals without using your own credit or money?

Don't work harder for someone else, when you can work smarter for yourself! (If someone had told me that before I got into real estate, I would have told them to mind their own business!) But you know what? Life circumstances change, priorities change, and sooner or later you've got to grow up and accept responsibility for your own life. That's what I finally did, after heartbreak and disappointment and having my life trashed by what amounted to ignorance on my part. If you think education is expensive, try ignorance!

There are a lot of real estate "gurus" out there. How is my boot camp different?

> **My system works** – It's as simple as that. First of all, of all the so-called experts out there, there are only three other teachers in this entire industry that I would recommend, other than myself. The rest are mostly hype, and don't really teach you how to make money in the real world. They just tell you what you want to hear, and pretty soon you realize you've been lied to. I don't do that. I use my own system to make money, day in and day out. That's how you know I'm for real.

> **The 20/80 rule** – I teach you what works all the time, with the least amount of work and in the fastest time. I teach you to be *productive*, not just *busy*.

> **This is the best investment of both your time and money** – It would cost you about $25,000 in seminars alone to learn even half of what I teach you in two days. Not to mention you'd have to attend at least five separate events lasting two to three days each! Just the travel expenses alone! My boot camp costs a fraction of what all the other boot camps cost, and you get to take home your own personal copy of my

system that includes a manual and a 16 cassette audio set.

> **I teach the boot camp personally** – I've been to real estate seminars where they play a video message from the "guru" who "couldn't make it", but his highly-trained instructor will teach you just as well. What a joke! I don't know about you, but I want to see a real, honest-to-goodness person in front of me that created the system and can answer any questions I might have.

> **I don't try to sell you other expensive boot camps** – This is how it works: I have one home study course, and I teach one live event. Combined, this is ALL the information you need to make a ton of money. I won't teach you just enough to sell you another boot camp like others do!

> **You won't needlessly spend unnecessary time and money listening to information that is stretched out to expand time** – They do this at some seminars to make you feel like you're getting your money's worth. I don't waste time putting you on a bus and touring houses or the local home improvement store. That's a complete waste of your time, and mine. There's no "filler" in my boot camp. It's hard, factual, practical information you can put to use as soon as you get home.

My boot camp walks you step-by-step through all the material listed in the Home Study Course, PLUS:

> **Personal Development** – I'll show you what I have done to achieve success, and where I learned it.

➤ **Dealing with Contractors** – I'll show you how to locate and retain qualified contractors that will get the job done
➤ **Setting up your business** – I'll show you how to conduct business without all the overhead. You don't need a fancy office, or a secretary or support staff. I made over $500,000 working part time by myself from a home office.
➤ **Perfecting the loan process** – I'll teach you how to become an expert at the loan process, including conventional and hard money loans. This alone will substantially increase your profits, because all the other investors just sign a contract with a buyer, and hope the deal closes. YOU will control this process!
➤ **And much, much more!**

You won't see me doing a boot camp every weekend like some of the other guru's. No way! It's too much work, and I don't like being away from my family. I do boot camps a few times a year at most; sometimes only twice a year. I do it in select cities. Remember, I make my real money doing actual real estate deals, not seminars or boot camps. And that's the lifestyle I'm going to keep!

Several seminar "gurus" have told me, "Chuck, break your system into numerous parts, and you'll make a ton of money." They've also told me not to include everything in one boot camp, but do several boot camps for $3,000 + each. Two of the top marketing experts in the country told me the same thing. I won't do it! I always hated it when I was a beginner and had just forked out $3,000 for a boot camp, only to discover that they're only teaching *part* of what you need to know. That's a real stretch and a disappointment to a hardworking person with a family to support who just maxed out their credit card to attend an event.

I don't want that! I want to hear that I really delivered a true value available nowhere else, and be able to HOLD MY HEAD UP HIGH! When I run into people who've attended my boot camp, I want to hear happy stories. You see, I started from where you are, and I know it takes some real guts to fork over money you can't afford. But I promise you it will be a decision you'll be glad you made.

My personal guarantee: sit in on the first day of the boot camp, and if you're not happy with the event, simply walk up to one of my people and ask for a refund! Also, you have up to one full year to repeat the boot camp at no extra charge. After the year is up, you can also repeat the event for a low, low price.

If you've already purchased my Home Study Course, you get to deduct the cost of that from the boot camp fee. To find out when my next boot camp is scheduled, log onto my website: http://www.chucksmithrealestateseminars.com or call 1-866-474-2432.

After reviewing Chuck Smith's manual and listening to... the accompanying cassette tapes, I strongly recommend this product... to beginning investors as well as experienced investors alike. As you will see, Chuck brings a unique background to his real estate investing business. I find him to be a man of integrity and a strong value system. Having met, and spent time with, Chuck and his wife Amy, it is easy to identify their unwavering dedication to each other, their children and their endeavors in real estate investing. Having worked with many students, both in group sessions and one on one, I found Chuck to be the most attentive, well prepared and his relentless determination is identifiable at every turn. Chuck's course is packed full of information... will not only serve you today, but in the upcoming years as a reference guide for forms, facts and the exact "how to's" for every real estate investor.

With kindest regards,

John F. Ulmer
The Westhaven Group

One-on-One Personal Coaching

If you're among the elite that are highly motivated, have a deep sense of urgency and want to achieve the highest level of success in real estate in the shortest time, you should consider my One-on-One Personal Coaching Program. It's expensive – as of this writing I charge $10,000 per day. But you get me as your *personal* teacher and mentor, which can cut years off your learning curve.

I take you by the hand, and show you the real ways to make money in this business without all the costly mistakes. I use a competency-based approach, and train my students through monitored learning experiences. This training can take place in my home town of Cleveland, Ohio, or your city – whichever you prefer.

Here's some things you need to consider before hiring *any* mentor or one-on-one coach:

1. **Is he or she a successful real estate investor –** and can they *prove* it? Anyone can read a few books and sound like an expert, but can they back up all their talk with proof like actual profit checks? Do they have successful students? Demand actual testimonials from real people, with names and cities, that have actually made money?

2. **Does this person still do real estate investing today?** You don't want someone who hasn't bought a house since 1980. You don't want someone that only teaches seminars all the time. Your one-on-one coach <u>must</u> understand **today's** real estate market before they can begin to teach you.

3. **Does this person have the ability to teach you?** And will they teach you *everything*, holding nothing

back? You don't need two days of war stories from some investor telling you how great they are. The only thing that matters is this: *when your person mentor leaves, can you make a lot of money consistently?*

I qualify on all three counts.

Will I teach just anybody? Absolutely NOT!

> ➢ If you're a "know it all" without an open mind, I won't waste the time training you. I don't have the time to waste, and you won't learn anything.
> ➢ If you are completely unmotivated, or have a bad attitude, I won't train you. Life is too short to waste it on people like you. I prefer to focus my time and energy on people who really want to change their lives!

Is there any preparation before a one-on-one coaching session? Yes. First I interview you on the phone *before* I agree to act as your personal coach. Then I send you an assessment package. This is a 50 + page questionnaire the helps me assess where you are, where you want to be in real estate, and what it will take to get you there. In addition, you have to have studied my "Quick Cash Ultimate Real Estate Investment Course" prior to my arrival for our one-on-one coaching session. This assures both of us time isn't wasted on information that you could have learned simply from studying the course.

To find out more about one-on-one personal coaching, log onto my website: http://www.chucksmithrealestateseminars.com or call 1-866-474-2432, or email me at csmith1758@aol.com.

> Chuck Smith has taken a myriad of concepts and boiled it down to a simple and easy to follow format that will make it easy for any beginner to follow the path to true wealth.
>
> *Lou Brown*
>
> Internationally known Author, Lecturer and Investor

That's it. I've tried to give you an idea of the struggles and triumphs I've faced and overcome. Life is a journey, and mine, like many others, has been filled with pitfalls and stumbles and some of the most amazing blessings anyone has every been gifted with.

My hope is that you can take some of these lessons to heart, and put them to good use in your own life with your own family and achieve the same sort of redemption and rebuilding that I've experienced. I couldn't ask for any more than that.

It's your future. It's in your hands.

Take Advantage of Affordable Legal Services

For 15 years I was a police officer and became intimately familiar with the legal system. I'm also an independent associate with Pre-Paid Legal Services. I've used this service for 7 years and have been involved with them as a side business for three years. I sell Pre-Paid Legal Services as an employee benefit to small and medium-sized companies around the country. I think it's the hottest employee benefit going and should be considered by every employer. Besides, if I would have known about this and had been a member when I was sued I wouldn't have lost a million dollars and filed for bankruptcy.

The American Bar Association (ABA), which most of the judges and lawyers in the United States belong to, has looked at Pre-Paid Legal Services. In many published articles about Pre-Paid Legal, the ABA is quoted as saying, "Americans have come to view the legal system as a necessity. The best way for the majority of Americans to be able to assure themselves of legal assistance when they need it is through a pre-paid legal plan." They didn't say a "pretty good" way. They said the *best* way!

Fortune, Forbes, USA Today and even the *Wall Street Journal* are all recommending the Pre-Paid Legal Services. Every year, *Forbes* ranks the 200 best small and medium–sized companies in the United States.

Pre-Paid Legal has been in the top 15 for the past five years in a row. It has also been ranked as the thirty-third fastest growing company on the New York Stock Exchange.

Are you worried about getting sued? You should be. You have a three times greater chance of being named in a legal action and going to court than you do of going to the hospital. And that statistic is about five years old. Chances are you have health insurance to cover health-related expenses. Where's your legal insurance?

The basic membership for Pre-Paid Legal is $26 a month. Your auto and health insurance have probably increased in the past five years, but Pre-Paid Legal's rates are not likely to change. The contract is for month to month, so you can sign up, try it out and cancel if you don't like it. However, I recommend that you keep it for at least a year to get some benefit from it.

Who's covered? You, your spouse and your children through college age (23 if they're still in school). You're covered throughout the entire United States. Pre-Paid Legal has 100,000 attorneys in its system using only the best attorneys in each state. That's how the service gets such good ratings.

Have you ever been overcharged for house or car repairs? You should have called Pre-Paid Legal. Ever had difficulty returning a product or service? You should have let your lawyer handle it. Ever gotten a traffic ticket? Pre-Paid Legal would have gone to court for you. Ever not gotten a security deposit back? Been audited? Bought a home, signed a contract or made a will? You need Pre-Paid Legal.

The service covers almost any legal need you could have in the areas of bankruptcy, criminal law and even real estate law. As a real estate investor, you'll have legal questions, so make it easy to get answers.

Pre-Paid Legal has been around for 30 years. It's a good company offering a product that works for a good value. Its coverage includes the following items:

- *Phone calls about legal issues.* Unlimited phone calls for personal or business questions. Lawyers usually charge $200 to $300 an hour. Most legal issues are dealt with through phone consultations
- *Letters.* If you have a case against someone, let the law firm write a letter with 50 lawyers' names across the top of it. "Take it off the credit report." "Insurance company, do the right thing." "Contractor, finish the job." Without Pre-Paid legal, it would cost you $200 to $300 to have an attorney a letter.
- *Contract Review.* Use this service any time you sign a contract such as a property purchase, car purchase, loan, cell phone agreement, employment agreement and so on.

Wealthy, smart families get their attorneys to look at all contracts before they sign them. How many contracts will you sign when you don't know exactly what you're signing?
- **_Wills._** Everyone needs a will. An estate-planning attorney charges $200 to $800 to draw up a will. I believe that everyone should have their wills written and Pre-Paid Legal Services can help you do this. I've told people to remember that it's only $26 a month. If you have children you need to have a will. If you don't like Pre-Paid Legal after you get your will done you can just cancel it. Please make your will. To get started go to **www.prepaidlegal.com/go/charlessmithjr** to find out about Pre-Paid Legal, or call our office, toll free at 1-866-474-2432.

Almost everyone has a hole in his or her insurance coverage. If you cause a bad car accident and someone dies as a result, you will be charged with involuntary manslaughter or vehicular homicide. Your car insurance will pay for medical bills and damage to your car, but it won't pay for criminal defense. Pre-Paid Legal Services was founded for this reason. Its lawyers will defend you if you're charged with vehicular homicide or manslaughter.

If you are sued, Pre-Paid Legal provides 75 hours a year of time from top attorneys to defend you. That's about $15,000 to $20,000 in the bank. That's enough to cover your defense for most of what you're involved in. If you are audited, Pre-Paid Legal provides up to 50 hours of tax attorney time. These are lawyers, not accountants. You can call and ask any legal tax question. Remember: don't use accountants to deal with the IRS; they don't have to follow the same confidentiality rules as attorneys do.

Instead of paying a high hourly rate for other legal work that may not be covered by Pre-Paid Legal, you get a discount rate of $150 an hour. For instance, if you have to sue someone, Pre-Paid Legal covers phone calls and letters, but if you have to go to court you'd be charged at a discounted rate.

Pre-Paid Legal Services also provides a form of legal shield. If the police pull you over a to question or detain you for a criminal matter, just being able to call your attorney seven days a week, 24 hours a day can help this or any other legal situation.

Listen, take my advice and become a member. I have used my membership numerous times and in one instance an attorney backed off from suing me because my provider law firm is the best in Ohio. I would not put my name and reputation on any service that was not the best.

DEFINITIONS OF REAL ESTATE TERMS

Acceleration clause

This is a clause in your mortgage which allows the lender to demand payment of the outstanding loan balance for a variety of reasons. The most common reason for accelerating a loan is if the borrower defaults on the loan or transfers title to another individual without informing the lender.

Adjustable Rate Mortgage (ARM)

This is a mortgage in which the interest changes periodically, according to fluctuations in an index.

Amortization

Your loan payment consists of two parts: interest and principal. A portion of your loan payment is used to pay accruing interest on a loan, while the remainder is applied to the principal. Over time, the interest portion decreases as the loan balance decreases, and the amount applied to principal increases so that the loan is paid off (amortized) in the specified time.

Annual percentage rate (APR)

This is <u>not</u> the rate on your loan. It is a value intended to reflect the true annual cost of borrowing, expressed as a percentage. (It was dreamed up by the government, so no wonder it's confusing!) In general terms, to figure out your APR - deduct the closing costs from your loan amount, then use your actual loan payment to calculate what the interest rate would be on that amount instead of your actual loan amount.

Application

The form used to apply for a mortgage loan. It contains information about a borrower's income, savings, assets, debts, and more.

Appraisal

A written document stating the value of a piece of property, based primarily on an analysis of comparable sales of similar homes nearby.

Appraised Value

This is a statement of a property's fair market value. It is based on an appraiser's knowledge, experience and training.

Appraiser

Someone qualified by education, training, and experience to estimate the value of real and personal property. Most appraisers operate independently, although some are employed by mortgage lenders.

Appreciation

The increase in the value of a property due to changes in market conditions, inflation, improvements, etc.

Assessed value

The valuation placed on property by a public tax assessor for purposes of taxation.

Asset

Any item of value owned by an individual or a company. Assets that can be quickly converted into cash are considered "liquid assets," such as bank accounts, stocks, bonds, mutual funds, etc. Other assets include real estate, personal property, and debts owed to you by someone else.

Assignment

When ownership of your mortgage is transferred from one company or individual to another, it is called an assignment.

Assumable Mortgage

This is a mortgage that can be assumed by the buyer when a home is sold. Usually, the borrower must "qualify" in order to assume the loan.

Balloon Mortgage

A mortgage loan that requires the remaining principal balance be paid at a specific point in time. For example, a loan may be amortized as if it would be paid over a thirty year period, but requires that at the end of the tenth year the entire remaining balance must be paid.

Balloon Payment

The final lump sum payment that is due at the end of a balloon mortgage.

Bankruptcy

Bankruptcy allows individuals or companies to restructure their debt or completely discharge it. There are strict federal guidelines relating to who can file bankruptcy and under what conditions.

Biweekly Mortgage

This is a type of mortgage in which you make payments every two weeks instead of once a month. Your extra payments reduce the principal much faster, substantially reducing the time it takes to pay off a thirty year mortgage.

Bridge Loan

Largely fallen out of favor, bridge loans were used by people who hadn't yet sold their previous property but need to close on a new property. The bridge loan became the down payment on the new property.

Broker

Broker has several definitions. Most Realtors are "agents" who work under a "broker," although some agents are brokers also, either working for themselves or under another broker. In the mortgage industry, broker usually refers to a company or individual that doesn't lend money for loans themselves, but arrange loans to larger lenders or investors.

Cap

Adjustable Rate Mortgages have fluctuating interest rates, but those fluctuations are usually limited to a certain amount. Those limitations may apply to how much the loan may adjust over a six month period, an annual period, and over the life of the loan, and are referred to as "caps."

Certificate of Deposit

A time deposit held in a bank which pays a fixed amount of interest to the depositor.

Certificate of Eligibility

This is a document issued by the Veterans Administration that certifies a veteran's eligibility for a VA loan.

Certificate of Reasonable Value (CRV)

Once the appraisal has been completed on a property being bought with a VA loan, the Veterans Administration issues a CRV.

Clear title
Any title to a property that is free of liens or legal questions as to ownership of the property.

Closing
Depending on the state you're in, this can mean different things. In some states a real estate transaction is not consider "closed" until the documents record at the local recorders office. In others, the "closing" is a meeting where all of the documents are signed and money changes hands.

Closing Costs
There are two types of closing costs: "non-recurring" and "pre-paid." Non-recurring closing costs are any items which are paid just once as a result of buying the property or obtaining a loan. "Pre-paids" are items which recur over time, such as property taxes and homeowners insurance.

Closing Statement
A statement that shows all of the costs deducted at the end of the sale.

Co-borrower

Any additional individual who is both obligated on the loan and is on title to the property.

Collateral
Something held as security against a loan. For a home loan, the property is the collateral. The borrower risks losing the property if the loan is not repaid according to the terms of the mortgage or deed of trust.

Commission
The fee that you pay to any of the sales professionals involved in each transaction, including but not limited to: Realtors, loan officers, title representatives, attorneys,

escrow agents, representatives for pest companies, home warranty companies, home inspection companies, insurance agents, and anyone else that can think of a way to jump in on your deal. Commissions are paid out of the charges paid by either the seller or buyer in the purchase transaction.

Common Area Assessments (CAM)

They're also know as Homeowners Association Fees. These are fees paid to the Homeowners Association by the owners of the individual units in a condominium or planned unit development (PUD) and are generally used to maintain the property and common areas.

Community property

In some states, any property acquired by a married couple during their marriage is considered to be owned jointly, except under very special and specific circumstances.

Comparable sales

Recent sales of similar properties in nearby areas and used to help determine the market value of a property. Also referred to as "comps."

Condominium

A type of ownership in real property where all of the owners own the property, common areas and buildings together, with the exception of the interior of the unit to which they have title. Often mistakenly referred to as a type of construction or development, it actually refers to the type of ownership.

Construction loan

A short-term, interim loan for the purpose of financing the cost of construction. The lender makes payments to the builder at periodic intervals for the work in progress.

Contingency
>A condition that must be met before a contract is legally binding. For example, home purchasers often include a contingency that specifies that the contract is not binding until the purchaser obtains a satisfactory home inspection report from a qualified home inspector.

Contract
>An oral or written agreement.

Conventional mortgage
>This refers to loans other than government loans (VA and FHA).

Credit history
>This is a record of an individual's repayment of debt. Credit histories are reviewed by mortgage lenders as one of the underwriting criteria in determining credit risk.

Creditor
>A person to whom money is owed.

Credit report
>A report of an individual's credit history prepared by a credit bureau and used by a lender in determining a loan applicant's creditworthiness.

Debt
>Any amount owed to another.

Deed
>The legal document conveying title to a property.

Deed of trust
>Some states, California for example, do not record mortgages. Instead, they record a deed of trust which is essentially the same thing.

Default
>This is failure to make the mortgage payment within a specified period of time. For first mortgages or first trust deeds, if a payment has still not been made within 30

days of the due date, the loan is considered to be in default.

Delinquency
Failure to make mortgage payments when mortgage payments are due. Even though they may not charge a "late fee" for a number of days, the payment is still considered to be late and the loan delinquent. If a loan payment is more than 30 days late, most lenders report the late payment to one or more credit bureaus.

Deposit
Generally, money given in advance of a larger amount being expected in the future. Often called in real estate as an "earnest money deposit."

Depreciation
This represents a decline in the value of property; the opposite of appreciation. Depreciation is also an accounting term which shows the declining monetary value of an asset and is used as an expense to reduce taxable income. Since this is not a real "out of pocket" expense where money is actually paid, lenders will add back depreciation expense for self-employed borrowers and count it as income.

Discount Points
In the mortgage industry, this term is usually used in reference to government loans, meaning FHA and VA loans. Discount points refer to any "points" paid in addition to the one percent loan origination fee. A "point" is one percent of the loan amount.

Down Payment
The part of the purchase price of a property that the buyer pays in cash and does not finance with a mortgage.

Due-on-sale provision
This is a clause in a mortgage that allows the lender to demand repayment in full if the borrower sells the property before the loan is due.

Earnest money deposit
This is a deposit made by the potential home buyer to show that he or she is serious about buying the house.

Easement
A right of way giving persons other than the owner access to, or over, a property.

Eminent domain
The right of a government to take private property for public use. Payment is due to the owner of its fair market value. Eminent domain is the basis for condemnation proceedings.

Encroachment
An improvement that intrudes illegally on someone else's property.

Encumbrance
Anything that affects or limits the title to a property, such as mortgages, leases, easements, or restrictions.

Equal Credit Opportunity Act (ECOA)
This is a federal law that requires lenders and other creditors to make credit equally available without discrimination based on race, color, religion, national origin, age, sex, marital status, or receipt of income from public assistance programs.

Equity
This is the difference between the fair market value of the property and the amount still owed on its mortgage and other liens.

Escrow

An item of value, money, or documents deposited with a third party to be delivered upon the fulfillment of a condition. For example, the earnest money deposit is put into escrow until delivered to the seller when the transaction is closed.

Escrow account

An escrow account or impound account is usually set up with your lender. This means the amount you pay each month includes a certain amount above what would be required if you were only paying your principal and interest. The extra money is held in your impound account (escrow account) for the payment of items like property taxes and homeowner's insurance when they come due.

Estate

The total of all the real property and personal property owned by an individual at the time of their death.

Eviction

The lawful expulsion of an occupant from real property.

Exclusive listing

A written contract that gives a licensed real estate agent the exclusive right to sell a property for a specified time.

Executor

A person named in a will to administer an estate. The court will appoint an administrator if no executor is named.

Fair Credit Reporting Act

A consumer protection law that regulates the disclosure of consumer credit reports by consumer/credit reporting agencies and establishes procedures for correcting mistakes on your credit record.

Fair market value
The highest price that a buyer is willing to pay, and the lowest a seller would accept.

Fannie Mae (FNMA)
The Federal National Mortgage Association, which is a congressionally chartered, shareholder-owned company that is the nation's largest supplier of home mortgage funds.

Federal Housing Administration (FHA)
This is an agency of the U.S. Department of Housing and Urban Development (HUD). Its primary purpose is insuring residential mortgage loans made by private lenders. The FHA sets standards for construction and underwriting but does not lend money, plan or construct housing.

FHA Mortgage
A mortgage that is insured by the Federal Housing Administration (FHA.)

First Mortgage
The mortgage that is in first place among any loans recorded against a property.

Fixed-rate mortgage
A mortgage in which the interest rate does not change during the entire term of the loan.

Foreclosure
The legal process by which a borrower in default under a mortgage loses his or her interest in the mortgaged property. This usually involves a forced sale of the property at public auction with the proceeds of the sale being applied to the mortgage debt.

Government National Mortgage Association (Ginnie Mae)

This is a government-owned corporation within the U.S. Department of Housing and Urban Development (HUD). Created by Congress on September 1, 1968, GNMA performs the same role as Fannie Mae and Freddie Mac in providing funds to lenders for making home loans. However, Ginnie Mae provides funds for government loans (FHA and VA).

Grantee

The person to whom an interest in real property is conveyed.

Grantor

The person conveying an interest in real property.

Hazard Insurance

Insurance coverage that in the event of physical damage to a property from fire, wind, vandalism, etc.

Home equity line of credit

A mortgage loan, usually as a second position, that allows the borrower to obtain cash drawn against the equity of his home, up to a predetermined amount.

Home Inspection

A thorough inspection by a professional that evaluates the structural and mechanical condition of a property. A satisfactory home inspection is often included as a contingency by the purchaser.

Homeowner's Warranty

This is a type of insurance often purchased by homebuyers that will cover repairs to certain items, such as heating or air conditioning, should they break down within the coverage period.

Joint tenancy
A form of ownership or taking title to property which means each party owns the whole property and that ownership is not separate. In the event of the death of one party, the survivor owns the property in its entirety.

Judgment
A decision made by a court of law. In judgments that require the repayment of a debt, the court may place a lien against the debtor's real property as collateral for the judgment's creditor.

Judicial foreclosure
A type of foreclosure proceeding used in some states that is handled as a civil lawsuit and conducted entirely under the auspices of a court. Other states use non-judicial foreclosure.

Late charge
The penalty a borrower must pay when a payment is not made on time. On a first trust deed or mortgage, this is usually when the payment is fifteen days overdue.

Lease
A written agreement between the property owner and a tenant that stipulates the payment and conditions under which the tenant may possess the real estate for a specified period of time.

Lease Option
An alternative financing option that allows home buyers to lease a home with an option to buy. Each month's rent payment include not only the rent, but an additional amount which can be applied toward the down payment on an already specified price.

Legal Description
A property description, recognized by law, that is sufficient to locate and identify the property.

Lender
A term which can refer to the institution making the loan or to the individual representing the firm. For example, loan officers are often referred to as "lenders."

Liabilities
A person's financial obligations. Liabilities include long-term and short-term debt, as well as any other amounts that are owed to others.

Liability insurance
This is Insurance coverage that offers protection against claims alleging that a property owner's negligence or inappropriate action resulted in bodily injury or property damage to another party. It is usually part of a homeowner's insurance policy.

Lien
A legal claim against a property that must be paid off when the property is sold. A mortgage or first trust deed is considered a lien.

Loan
A sum of money (principal) that is borrowed, and is generally repaid with interest.

Loan Officer
Also know as a lender, loan representative, loan "rep," account executive, and others. The loan officer serves several functions and has various responsibilities: they solicit loans, are representatives of the lending institution, and they represent the borrower to the lending institution.

Loan Origination
How a lender refers to the process of obtaining new loans.

Loan-to-value (LTV)

The percentage relationship between the amount of the loan and the appraised value or sales price (whichever is lower).

Lock-in

An agreement in which the lender guarantees a specified interest rate for a certain amount of time at a certain cost.

Maturity

The date on which the principal balance of a loan, bond, or other financial instrument becomes due and payable.

Mortgage

A legal document that pledges a property to the lender as security for payment of a debt. Instead of mortgages, some states use First Trust Deeds.

Mortgage Insurance (MI)

This is insurance that covers the lender against some of the losses incurred as a result of a default on a home loan. Often mistakenly referred to as PMI, which is actually the name of one of the larger mortgage insurers, mortgage insurance is usually required in one form or another on all loans that have a loan-to-value higher than eighty percent.

Multi-dwelling units

Properties that provide separate housing units for more than one family, although they secure only a single mortgage.

No-cost Loan

Many lenders offer loans that you can obtain at "no cost." You need to find out if this means there are no "lender" costs associated with the loan, or if it also covers the other costs you would normally have in a purchase or refinance transactions, such as title insurance, escrow fees, settlement fees, appraisal, recording fees, notary fees, and others.

Note
A legal document that obligates a borrower to repay a mortgage loan at a stated interest rate during a specified period of time.

Notice of default
A formal written notice to a borrower that a default has occurred and that legal action may be taken.

Owner Financing
A property purchase in which the property seller provides all or part of the financing.

PITI
This stands for principal, interest, taxes and insurance. If you have an "impounded" loan, then your monthly payment to the lender includes all of these and probably includes mortgage insurance as well. If you do not have an impounded account, then the lender still calculates this amount and uses it as part of determining your debt-to-income ratio.

Point
A point is 1 percent of the amount of the mortgage.

Power of attorney
This is a legal document that authorizes another person to act on your behalf. A power of attorney can grant complete authority or can be limited to certain acts and/or certain periods of time.

Pre-approval
A loosely used term which is generally taken to mean that a borrower has completed a loan application and provided debt, income, and savings documentation which an underwriter has reviewed and approved. A pre-approval is usually done at a certain loan amount and

making assumptions about what the interest rate will actually be at the time the loan is actually made, as well as estimates for the amount that will be paid for property taxes, insurance and others. A pre-approval applies only to the borrower. Once a property is chosen, it must also meet the underwriting guidelines of the lender. Contrast with pre-qualification

Prepayment

Any amount paid to reduce the principal balance of a loan before the due date. Payment in full on a mortgage that may result from a sale of the property, the owner's decision to pay off the loan in full, or a foreclosure. In each case, prepayment means payment occurs before the loan has been fully amortized.

Prepayment penalty

A fee that may be charged to a borrower who pays off a loan before it is due.

Pre-qualification

This usually refers to the loan officer's written opinion of the ability of a borrower to qualify for a home loan, after the loan officer has made inquiries about debt, income, and savings. The information provided to the loan officer may have been presented verbally or in the form of documentation, and the loan officer may or may not have reviewed a credit report on the borrower.

Principal

The amount borrowed or remaining unpaid. The part of the monthly payment that reduces the remaining balance of a mortgage.

Promissory note

A written promise to repay a specified amount over a specified period of time.

Public auction
   A sale, held in an announced public location to sell property to repay a mortgage that is in default.
Purchase agreement
   A written contract signed by the buyer and seller stating the terms and conditions under which a property will be sold.
Qualifying ratios
   Calculations that are used in determining whether a borrower can qualify for a mortgage. There are two ratios. The "top" or "front" ratio is a calculation of the borrower's monthly housing costs (principle, taxes, insurance, mortgage insurance, homeowner's association fees) as a percentage of monthly income. The "back" or "bottom" ratio includes housing costs as will as all other monthly debt.

Quitclaim deed
A deed that transfers without warranty whatever interest or title a grantor may have at the time the conveyance is made.

Real Estate Agent
A person licensed to negotiate and transact the sale of real estate.

Real Estate Settlement Procedures Act (RESPA)
A consumer protection law that requires lenders to give borrowers advance notice of closing costs.

Real property
Land and appurtenances, including anything of a permanent nature such as structures, trees, minerals, and the interest, benefits, and inherent rights thereof.

Realtor®
A real estate agent, broker or an associate who holds active membership in a local real estate board that is affiliated with the National Association of Realtors.

Recorder
The public official who keeps records of transactions that affect real property in the area. Sometimes known as a "Registrar of Deeds" or "County Clerk."

Recording
The act of noting in the registrar's office of the details of a properly executed legal document, such as a deed, a mortgage note, a satisfaction of mortgage, or an extension of mortgage, thereby making it a part of the public record.

Refinance transaction
The process of paying off one loan with the proceeds from a new loan using the same property as security.

Repayment plan
An arrangement made to repay delinquent installments or advances.

Right of First Refusal
A provision in an agreement that requires the owner of a property to give another party the first opportunity to purchase or lease the property before he or she offers it for sale or lease to others.

Right of Ingress or Egress
The right to enter or leave designated premises.

Right of survivorship
In joint tenancy, the right of survivors to acquire the interest of a deceased joint tenant.

Second mortgage
A mortgage that has a lien position subordinate to the first mortgage.

Secured loan
A loan that is backed by collateral.

Security
The property that will be pledged as collateral for a loan.

Seller carry-back
An agreement in which the owner of a property provides financing, often in combination with an assumable mortgage.

Survey
A drawing or map showing the precise legal boundaries of a property, the location of improvements, easements, rights of way, encroachments, and other physical features.

Sweat equity
Contribution to the construction or rehabilitation of a property in the form of labor or services rather than cash.

Tenancy in common
> As opposed to joint tenancy, when there are two or more individuals on title to a piece of property, this type of ownership does not pass ownership to the others in the event of death.

Third-party origination
> A process by which a lender uses another party to completely or partially originate, process, underwrite, close, fund, or package the mortgages it plans to deliver to the secondary mortgage market.

Title
> A legal document evidencing a person's right to or ownership of a property.

Title Company
> A company that specializes in examining and insuring titles to real estate.

Title insurance
> Insurance that protects the lender (lender's policy) or the buyer (owner's policy) against loss arising from disputes over ownership of a property.

Title search
> A check of the title records to ensure that the seller is the legal owner of the property and that there are no liens or other claims outstanding.

Transfer of ownership
> Any means by which the ownership of a property changes hands. Lenders consider all of the following situations to be a transfer of ownership: the purchase of a property "subject to" the mortgage, the assumption of the mortgage debt by the property purchaser, and any exchange of possession of the property under a land sales contract or any other land trust device.

Transfer tax
State or local tax payable when title passes from one owner to another.

Truth-in-Lending
A federal law that requires lenders to fully disclose, in writing, the terms and conditions of a mortgage, including the annual percentage rate (APR) and other charges.

Two- to four-family property
A property that consists of a structure that provides living space (dwelling units) for two to four families, although ownership of the structure is evidenced by a single deed.

Trustee
A fiduciary who holds or controls property for the benefit of another.

VA mortgage
A mortgage that is guaranteed by the Department of Veterans Affairs (VA).

Vested
Having the right to use a portion of a fund such as an individual retirement fund. For example, individuals who are 100 percent vested can withdraw all of the funds that are set aside for them in a retirement fund. However, taxes may be due on any funds that are actually withdrawn.

Veterans Administration (VA)
An agency of the federal government that guarantees residential mortgages made to eligible veterans of the military services. The guarantee protects the lender against loss and thus encourages lenders to make mortgages to veterans.

REFERENCE SECTION

I've made personal development and growth a priority in my life. These are a few of the books, systems and programs that I've studied, and that have helped me immensely. This list is by no means all-inclusive, but I've found that these struck a chord with me. I urge you to study these, then embark on your own journey. Find the teachers that resonate with you and continue learning and growing. I promise you, it will be well worth the time and effort invested.

Lead the Field
By Earl Nightingale   http://www.nightingale.com

Personal Power
By Tony Robbins   http://www.personalpower.com

How to Win Friends and Influence People
By Dale Carnegie   http://www.dale-carnegie.com

The 48 Laws of Power
By Robert Greene   available from major book retailers everywhere

Think and Grow Rich
By Napoleon Hill   available from major book retailers everywhere

Work Less, Make More
By Jennifer White   available from major book retailers everywhere

Rich Dad, Poor Dad
   By Robert Kiyosaki   http://www.richdadsseminars.com

Time Tactics of Very Successful People
   By B. Eugene Griessman available from major book
                                             retailers everywhere

What it Takes to Be Number 1
   By Vince Lombardi, Jr.   available from major book
                                             retailers everywhere

The 25 Sales Habits of Highly Successful Salespeople
   By Stephen Schiffman   available from major book
                                             retailers everywhere

The Art of War (any edition)
   By Sun-Tzu   available from major book
                                             retailers everywhere

Ron LeGrand   http://www.ronlegrand.com
                                        1-904-262-0491

Creating Wealth; Nothing Down
   By Robert G. Allen   available from major book
                                             retailers everywhere

How to have Confidence and Power in Dealing with People
   By Les Giblin   available from major book
                                             retailers everywhere

INDEX

A

Abraham Lincoln, 137
asset protection, 41, 42, 46,
    115, 116, 117, 118, 120,
    121, 122, 124, 125, 126,
    127, 129, 130, 131
Asset Protection System,
    149

B

bankruptcy, xxiv, xxv, 44, 46,
    48, 160
boot camp, 46, 53, 100, 142,
    149, 150, 151, 152, 153
boot camps, 45, 46, 48, 52,
    53, 150, 151, 152
Building a Buyers List, 71
Building and Cultivating a
    Buyers List, 72, 147
Buying Properties "Subject
    To", 86

C

Chief of Police, 23
Cleveland, ii, xxiii, xxvi, 2, 3,
    5, 6, 7, 8, 9, 19, 33, 34, 45,
    46, 72, 74, 108, 155
cocaine, 9, 10, 11
continuing education, 48
Contract Assigning, 84, 85,
    145
Contract Assignment, 147

contract assignments, 50
cop, i, iii, ix, xxiii, xxiv, 2, 5, 7,
    8, 9, 12, 13, 17, 18, 20, 26,
    28, 35, 138, 148
Cop, 3
Cops, 12, 20
Corporation, 119
Crack, 11

D

DEFINITIONS OF REAL
    ESTATE TERMS, 158
Discounting a Mortgage, 92

F

FBI, 19, 20
fixer-uppers, 34, 35, 88
Flipping, v

G

Getting the Deed, 146, 148

H

home study course, 46, 47,
    100, 151
Home Study Course, 106,
    143, 149, 151, 153

I

injuries, xxiv, 18, 19, 108
inspection, 35, 36, 162, 163,
    169

Internal Affairs, 28
Irrevocable Children's Trust,
130
Irrevocable Life Insurance
Trust, 128

J

Joint Ownership, 117
junkers, 33

L

Land Trust, 86, 88, 127
landlord, 22, 32, 34, 37, 46,
50, 63, 64, 145
Lease Options, 148
Limited Liability Company
(LLC, 124
Limited Partnership, 121
Living Trust, 125

M

Magnetic Marketing for Real
Estate Investors ®, 148
Magnetic Marketing System,
76

O

One-on-One Personal
Coaching, 155
Owner Financing, 89, 148

P

Partnerships, 121

personal development, 48,
132, 138, 141, 179
pretty house, 35
Private Lenders for Real
Estate Investors ®, 148
private money, 80

Q

Quick Cash Ultimate Real
Estate Boot Camp, 100,
149
Quick Cash Ultimate Real
Estate Investment System,
69, 100, 146
Quick Turning, v

R

REFERENCE SECTION,
179
Retailing, 95, 145, 147

S

Sandwich leases, 146
Schematic Diagrams, 148
Seller Financing, 91
Slum landlords, 34
Sole Proprietorship, 117
student's success stories,
101
Subject To, 86, 87, 88, 89,
90
sued, xxiv, 38, 39, 40, 41, 84,
115, 116, 120, 121, 122,
129, 130
SWAT team, 7, 24, 25

T

Tough Cop Contractor
   Management System ®,
   148

U

Umbrella Policy, 129

W

wholesaling, 50, 145
Wholesaling, 145, 147

Y

years on the force, 7

From Cop to CEO

"This book is full of practical, proven, step-by-step strategies, methods and techniques you can use IMMEDIATELY to make an ENORMOUS amount of money in real estate. Chuck Smith's ideas are worth a fortune." –Brian Tracy, best selling author

"Chuck Smith's story is truly an amazing one. If this doesn't get you motivated you may want to check your pulse." –G. William Barnett, best selling author of *Are You Dumb Enough to Be Rich*

"This book has the action and drama of a blockbuster movie! The true story of Chuck Smith, a tough street cop, the fortune he earned, then lost thru lack of knowledge, then REGAINED by learning from his losses. You can now profit from his true story. This book may INSPIRE you or it may INFURIATE you, but it will not leave you the same! The author reminds us we are responsible for our own lot in life! If you want to change your life (for the better) READ this book! I highly recommend it." -John Abbott, best selling author of *Secrets of Real Estate Millionaires*

"I have watched Chuck Smith go from a low paid street cop to a world class real estate entrepreneur making $500,000 per year almost over night. This book is his story. It is a straight to the point masterpiece worth its weight in gold. Consider yourself lucky Chuck is about to enter your life." -Ron LeGrand, America's Quick Turn Master and Millionaire Maker

"I have been a successful investor for over 30 years and have made millions. Never before have I seen such a powerful system, which is proven to work for all that implement it! The serious new and seasoned real estate investor MUST read this book! Chuck Smith teaches how to make money immediately." -Jim Hughes, best selling author of *Privacy and Asset Protection-A Primer* and President of Midwest REIA Chicago, IL

"I traveled all the way from London, England to Cleveland, Ohio to study personally under Chuck Smith. His system even works here." -Dr. Keith Roachford, London, England

Printed in the United States
26012LVS00002B/70-1008

9 781591 134145